World Food Café

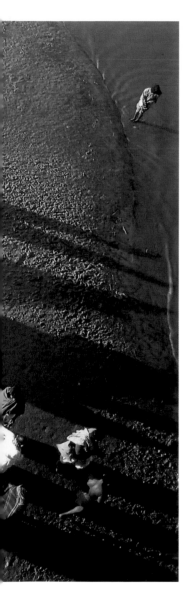

World
Food
Café

Chris & Carolyn Caldicott

Recipe photography by James Merrell

FRANCES LINCOLN

For Nicholas

Frances Lincoln Limited
4 Torriano Mews
Torriano Avenue
London NW5 2RZ

World Food Café

British Library Cataloguing in Publication data
A catalogue record for this book is available
from the British Library

Printed in Hong Kong

ISBN   0 7112 1440 9

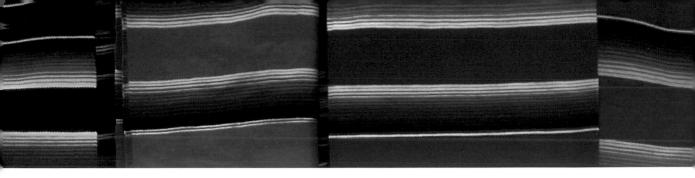

Contents

INTRODUCTION 6

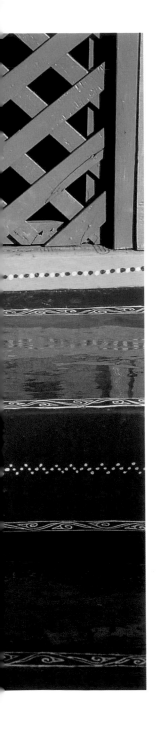

INTRODUCTION

Ten years of travelling the world in search of images and stories as a freelance photojournalist and as the Expedition Photographer-in-Residence at London's Royal Geographical Society have given me a wealth of memorable experiences. Not the least of these have involved the diverse and delicious meals I have been privileged to eat in generous people's homes and remote expedition camps, at simple street stalls and fashionable restaurants, and in dozens of countries. I started to collect recipes whenever possible, in the hope of being able to reproduce the best at home.

In 1989 I met Carolyn, already an accomplished cook, who similarly found discovering and eating exotic foods one of the greatest pleasures of travel. We began travelling together, visiting Africa, the Middle East, the Indian subcontinent, Southeast Asia, and Central and South America, accumulating ideas for globally inspired recipes with the aim of one day opening a restaurant in which we could serve all our favourite dishes from around the world. Some of the recipes we gathered from people we met along the way who were kind enough to invite us into their homes to eat or stay with them, others are traditional dishes of specific regions. Some have been worked out by observing the skills of speedy chefs in busy pavement cafés on crowded city streets, still others patiently demonstrated by local people in jungles and deserts and on mountains — some of the world's remote places, where with so few distractions, food, especially the evening meal, is a very necessary pleasure.

As both Carolyn and I travelled as vegetarians we were used to the challenge of finding good things to eat in places where the traditional cuisine lends itself more naturally to meat or seafood. Although this is rarely a serious problem, there have been times when we felt we were missing out on some exciting dishes simply because they were never made meatless. In such cases we adapted the traditional recipe, replacing the meat or fish with suitable alternatives to produce vegetarian versions just as tasty, with all the flavours and tastes so evocative of distant lands.

The freshly washed front doorstep of a house in Orissa in eastern India

Introduction

In 1991 we opened the World Food Café in London. The opportunity came when our friend and co-founder Nicholas Sanders offered us a 56 square metre (600 sq ft) room on the first floor of a building he was restoring in Neal's Yard in Covent Garden. The building had previously been used as an animation studio by the Monty Python comedy team before being burnt to the ground in an accidental fire. Nicholas was in the process of rebuilding it in its original exterior style, and filling it with new businesses. Our space had no plumbing, electricity or gas — not even a floor: just four walls and three wonderful huge windows opening out on to the tree-filled peace of Neal's Yard. We wanted the café to retain this bright, open character, to provide an appealing place where we could serve meals made up from a variety of dishes from the countries we had visited. With the opportunity to design the interior from scratch, we were able to organize it so that most of the seating is around an open-plan kitchen providing customers with a view of their food being prepared; a large table under each of the three windows enables groups of up to ten to sit together. The café is also a perfect venue to exhibit photographs taken on each trip, and to play compilations of music originating from as many countries as the food.

ABOUT THE RECIPES

The recipes in this book can all be easily cooked at home with the right ingredients; where these might be difficult to find we have suggested alternatives. Some of the dishes are those we serve every day in the World Food Café; others make only occasional appearances there. In the café the food is usually cooked without dairy products; cheeses, yoghurts and creams are offered as optional garnishes. Meat and fish are never used. In this book we have indicated some of the recipes that would traditionally use fish or seafood.

Spices both aromatic and hot are a common ingredient of food from the countries represented in this book. In certain extreme cases we have eaten dishes that were distinctive for an ability to induce almost hallucinogenic states of delirium, as cocktails of pounded chillies, garlic and ginger released their power and left mouths on fire, brows moist and heads reeling. Any pleasure derived from this level of spicing is a very personal one, not universally shared. We have tried to achieve moderation in the use of chillies, and quantities may be reduced

Top to bottom **Chinese characters on a red wall in Malaysia; a honey**

8

stall in Oaxaca, Mexico;
a dhow at sunset in
Zanzibar

or increased according to taste. A number of dishes contain lots of spices other than chillies: these combine in specific amounts to form complex and unique flavours and therefore should not be altered as freely as the chilli quantities. Some of the food in this book is a little more spiced than we would normally pitch it for consumption in the café, reflecting our own passion for more authentic levels of spicing.

Rice is another ingredient that requires some personal choice. Our own preference at home is to use white Indian basmati rice, which has a distinctive aroma and taste. In the café we always use brown long-grain rice, usually Italian or American, which the customers seem to prefer. Both brown and white rice work well with any of the dishes. Basmati rice does come in a brown version, and there are dozens of other types available both brown and white, long- and short-grain, and organic — it's simply a case of choosing your favourite.

Another aspect of eating in most of the countries we have visited is the serving of several dishes at a time. In the café we have adopted this custom so that when we serve a plate of food from a particular country we include, alongside, a selection of salsas, salads, chutneys, pickles, sambols, sambals, dals, raitas, rice and bread, depending on the dish's origins. Recipes for many of these accompaniments are included in the following chapters so that meals can be constructed from different combinations of them.

The book is divided up geographically into four chapters and does not pretend to be a comprehensive guide to the cuisine of the regions covered, but rather reflects our personal choice of dishes enjoyed in areas we have explored. The first chapter covers Morocco and Egypt north of the Sahara, leading into Jordan and the Levant and on to Turkey and Oman; south of the Sahara we visit Mali in West Africa, then Tanzania, Kenya and Zanzibar in East Africa, and finally the island of La Digue in the Indian Ocean. The second chapter is dedicated to India, Nepal and Sri Lanka. The third deals with other countries we have visited in Asia, starting with Burma, heading north to China, and then down through Southeast Asia including Laos, Thailand, Malaysia, Borneo and Bali. In the final chapter we take a circuitous route through South and Central America, from Brazil through Bolivia, Peru and Ecuador, then to Costa Rica and Mexico, and ending with the Caribbean island of Cuba.

The Middle East

& Africa

The Middle East & Africa

This chapter covers a vast area of the globe, from the Atlantic coast of West Africa across the continent to the Indian Ocean and over the Arabian peninsula to the shores of the Gulf. We start with Africa north of the Sahara Desert.

Morocco is a land of bountiful good food. Tajine stews — interesting concoctions of fresh vegetables, fruits, herbs and spices — are served with hot harissa pastes, fluffy couscous and nutty breads. There are thick soups and crunchy salads. And any of these may be eaten in such exotic locations as a winding medieval souk (marketplace), a fortified Atlantic port, a crumbling village in the Atlas Mountains, or a desert camp among Saharan dunes.

Farther east along the Mediterranean, in Egypt, a style of eating begins that varies little through Jordan and the Levant. There is less use of fresh vegetables and an increasing use of pulses, salads and purées — many excellent, and most vegetarian. In fact a travelling vegetarian can find something to eat in almost any street café from Aswan to Aleppo, the only drawback being that it will probably be the same in each one. Eventually the influences of Turkey to the north or Iran to the east begin to take over.

Turkish food, like that of the Levantine countries, is often served as a meze, or plate, containing lots of different salads, purées, sauces, pickles and bread, with the increased fertility of the Mediterranean's north shore providing an increasing choice of fresh vegetable ingredients.

Turkey shares with most of the Middle East a tradition of eating the very un-vegetarian dish of *mensaf*, which uses a whole sheep. In the oil-rich cities of the Gulf you are as likely to have to suffer bland fast food as *mensaf*. However, in Oman we found some very interesting dishes made in an Iranian style using rose water, nuts and dates, as well as excellent Indian curry houses catering to the migrant workers who seem to keep the country going.

In sub-Saharan Africa, despite the variety of cultures and landscapes over such a large area, the variety of cuisines can be rather limited, although there are memorable exceptions. Travelling around many of the forty or so countries between the Sahara and the Cape of Good Hope can be hard work, especially for vegetarians. Even confirmed carnivores, reduced to a diet of little more than boiled goat and maize-meal for days on end, can become desperate for a little variety. Our most memorable meals have been found in the desert fringes and delta lands of West Africa, and around the Somali coast of East Africa.

Pages 10-11 **The migration of Fulani cattle across the Niger River at Diafarabe**

Above **A bowl of succulent red olives in a Morrocan souk**
Above right **The great mud mosque at Djenné in Mali**

The cooking traditions of the Ethiopian highlands lend themselves well to vegetarian dishes, although in practice the lack of meat is more often due to economic circumstances than to personal choice. Foreign influences, such as the fiery piri-piri sauces of southern Africa's ex-Portuguese colonies or the rich savoury sauces of the Malay community on the South African Cape, often provide variety.

West African cooking is peppery, dominated by okra, sweet potatoes, plantain, ginger, cayenne and groundnuts. Being vegetarian there was rarely a problem, although finding anything to eat at all sometimes was. Extraordinary landscapes and friendly people are welcome distractions from hunger.

The dishes of East Africa's Somali coast and Zanzibar rely on spicy, fresh coconut milk sauces and seafood (which may be replaced by beans and vegetables if desired). In Ethiopia an earthy *berberé* mixture of rough-ground spices flavours lentil and vegetable stews eaten with wholesome breads.

Somewhere out in the Indian Ocean, between the Arabian peninsula and the coast of East Africa, a cocktail of Arab, African, Asian and European traditions has been blended to create the Creole dishes of the Seychelles islands — providing some of the most exciting recipes in this chapter. The tiny island of La Digue where we spent our time enjoying these is the most idyllic and beautiful place we stayed in all our travels.

MOROCCO

Moroccan cooking is a blend of traditions. From the Berbers came tajines, or slow-cooked stews; harira, a hearty soup; and couscous, the North African staple — grains of semolina with a fine coating of wheat flour, perfectly preserved until brought to life by steam and oil, and thus ideal for long desert journeys. Bedouin Arabs introduced dried pastas, dates and bread. More succulent additions of olives, olive oil, nuts, apricots and herbs came from the Andalusian Moors. All this, mixed with spices from the Orient, and a final French influence to give some finishing touches — such as fresh-baked baguette every morning — and Morocco couldn't go wrong. Even strict vegetarians find plenty of good things to eat, while if you don't mind a bit of lamb stock here and there it is very easy to eat in places such as the atmospheric night markets. When cooking at home the results can be just as delicious avoiding meat altogether.

We ate well in the markets and cafés while travelling, but the real privilege was spending time with the cooks in houses we stayed in. We were photographing beautiful houses in Marrakesh and Ouarzazate that are let out as holiday villas. Each house has a resident cook, and as we could only work in daylight we were free to spend the evenings watching and helping the cooks to prepare our evening meals, and to work out ways of keeping them meatless.

In Marrakesh, one of these houses was hidden deep in the medina, the old Arab quarter, of the city. A pair of weathered wooden doors in a dusty alley opened on to a vast courtyard filled with palms, fountains and a swimming pool and surrounded by pillared verandas shading elegant interiors. Sitting on the sumptuous cushions scattered around the flat roof, we were afforded superb views over the rooftops of the old city. One evening the owner invited several friends to meet us, and we were soon immersed in lively conversation. Some snacks appeared from the kitchen, among them piping hot *briouats* — small pastry envelopes stuffed with a filling. They tasted good but unusual. Carolyn asked what the filling was and understood it to be Brie, which made sense as the taste was milky and the owner was French. As the evening progressed we ate more and more of these. When we arrived for breakfast the next morning — feeling somewhat uncomfortable from the excesses of the night before — we complimented the cook on the *briouats*. She exclaimed, 'Did Madame not tell you they were filled with puréed brain?' She then attempted to reassure us by saying, 'Don't worry — we have not the mad cow disease here yet.' This did little to stop us feeling even more uncomfortable. All the dishes in this chapter are completely brain-free, and delicious.

An olive stall in the
Marrakesh souk

Mint tea is drunk in all the Moroccan pavement cafés, mainly frequented by men. It is unusual to see women in these places, unless they are of dubious morals. Tea is served in sturdy glasses, poured from a silver pot, and is usually very sweet. Traditionally it is made from gunpowder green tea; we also like it with Darjeeling, as it then needs little, if any, sugar.

MINT TEA

Makes 6 small glasses
    2 teaspoons gunpowder green tea or
       Darjeeling
    6 sprigs of mint
  sugar or honey to taste

Make tea in the conventional manner in a large pot, add the mint and allow to brew for about 5 minutes. Serve hot or chilled, with added sugar or honey to taste.

HARIRA SOUP

SERVES 4–6

5 tablespoons olive oil
2 red onions, diced
2 garlic cloves, crushed
handful of flat-leaf parsley, chopped
1 teaspoon ground ginger
1 teaspoon coarsely ground black
  pepper
½ teaspoon ground saffron or
  turmeric
½ teaspoon cayenne pepper
1 tablespoon paprika
1 teaspoon ground coriander
2 medium potatoes, diced
3 carrots, diced

4 celery stalks, diced
125 g/4 oz green lentils
2 tablespoons tomato purée
450 g/1 lb tomatoes, puréed in a
  food processor
600 ml/1 pint stock
225 g/8 oz cooked or drained
  canned chickpeas
60 g/2 oz cooked or drained canned
  white beans
125 g/4 oz vermicelli, broken up
juice of 1 lemon
salt

Heat the oil in a large saucepan. When it is hot, fry the onions and garlic until they soften.

Add the parsley, ginger, black pepper, saffron or turmeric, cayenne, paprika and ground coriander, stirring to prevent sticking. Then add the potatoes, carrots and celery, green lentils and tomato purée. Stir well and add the puréed fresh tomatoes, stock and enough water to cover all the ingredients well. Bring to the boil, reduce the heat and simmer for 45 minutes, adding more water when necessary (pulses do soak up a lot of water during cooking). The general aim is for a thickish soup.

Now add the cooked chickpeas, white beans and vermicelli and cook for a further 5 minutes, or until the vermicelli are soft. Finally pour in the lemon juice and season to taste.

By day the main square in Marrakesh, the Djmaa el-Fna, is the haunt of colourful snake-charmers, water-sellers and trinket-sellers; as night falls out come the story-tellers, fire-eaters, acrobats and magicians, who provide entertainment among the rows of open-air food-stalls lit by blazing kerosene lanterns. Customers sit at simple wooden tables on long benches and choose portions of whatever takes their fancy from the mounds of tempting food on display.

There are lots of different recipes for harira soup. We ate this version as an early snack before dinner in the night market, where it is served from huge pans and eaten with wooden spoons. Some stalls sell nothing but harira soup, and become very busy during the Islamic fasting month of Ramadan, when a bowl of harira is a popular way to break the day's fast.

The atmospheric night market in Marrakesh

MARRAKESH TAJINE

SERVES 4–6

5 tablespoons olive oil

2 red onions, thinly sliced

1 level tablespoon coarsely ground black pepper

1 heaped teaspoon ground cumin

½ teaspoon ground saffron or turmeric

1 teaspoon ground cinnamon

1 aubergine, cut in half lengthwise, then sliced into 1 cm/½ inch half-rounds

4 small potatoes, cut into quarters

1 large sweet potato, chopped into large chunks

1 red and 1 green pepper, deseeded and cut lengthwise into 2.5 cm/1 inch strips

salt

6 artichoke hearts (fresh or canned)

125 g/4 oz fine green beans

4 medium tomatoes, peeled and roughly chopped

1 tablespoon tomato purée

handful of flat-leaf parsley, chopped, plus more to garnish

handful of coriander leaves, chopped, plus more to garnish

small handful of raisins

small handful of dried apricots

85 g/3 oz stoned olives

harissa (page 22), to serve

crunchy baguette or couscous, to serve

Heat the oil in a large saucepan and, when hot, fry the onions until they start to soften.

Add the spices, stirring to prevent sticking. Add the aubergine, potatoes, sweet potato and green and red peppers. Sprinkle with a little salt as this helps prevent the aubergine from absorbing all the oil.

When the aubergine starts to soften, add all the remaining vegetables and the tomato purée with just enough water barely to cover the vegetables. Add the parsley, coriander, raisins, apricots and olives. Bring to the boil and simmer gently until all the vegetables are really soft and the sauce is reduced until it is thick and rich, with the oil returning on the top.

Garnish with lots of parsley and coriander, and serve with harissa and crunchy baguette or couscous.

The Marrakesh markets are full of every imaginable herb, spice and dried fruit, and we found that tajines tend to be much richer there than elsewhere in Morocco. We watched a sixty-year-old chef cook this tajine in the heart of the medina. Vegetables are cooked slowly and are served very soft, almost crumbling into the sauce. They are cut in large pieces to prevent them from disintegrating completely.

Marrakesh Tajine

OUARZAZATE COUSCOUS

Serves 4–6

5 tablespoons olive oil

2 red onions, sliced from top to bottom into 4 wedges

1 large handful of flat-leaf parsley, chopped, plus more to garnish

3 tomatoes, skinned and roughly chopped

½ teaspoon ground saffron or turmeric

1 teaspoon ground ginger

1 teaspoon ground cumin

1 teaspoon coarsely ground black pepper

6 small carrots

6 small turnips, halved if large

1 small white cabbage (about 450 g/ 1 lb), cut into six lengthwise

600 ml/1 pint stock

1 preserved lemon (page 22)

450 g/1 lb pumpkin, peeled, deseeded and cut into large cubes

6 small courgettes, part peeled lengthwise to create a striped effect

salt

harissa (page 22), to serve (optional)

For the couscous

450 g/1 lb fine couscous

600 ml/1 pint boiling water

large knob of butter

125 g/4 oz toasted flaked almonds

ground cinnamon

In a large heavy-based saucepan, heat the oil and fry the onion until it starts to soften. Then add the parsley, tomatoes and spices. Stir to avoid sticking. Add the carrots, turnips and cabbage, and fry to soften.

Add the stock and the preserved lemon. If necessary, add more water so the vegetables are nearly covered in liquid. Bring to the boil, cover and simmer for 15 minutes. Add the pumpkin and the courgettes. Simmer for another 10–15 minutes or so, until all the vegetables are very soft, adding more water if needed. The end result should be quite soupy.

While the vegetables are cooking you can prepare the couscous: place the couscous in a large bowl, add the boiling water and leave to stand for 10 minutes. Now fluff the couscous with a fork or with your fingers until the grains are separated. To keep it warm, either sprinkle with water, cover and leave in a preheated low oven; or, if you have a steamer, steam on top of the vegetables for 10 minutes prior to serving.

We spent a few days in an amazing house overlooking a huge lake on the edge of the desert between the High Atlas and the Anti-Atlas mountains. Only a few miles along the Dades valley was an impressive collection of grand kasbahs (citadels) set among lush palmeraies in the oasis of Skoura. The house was very remote, but the wonderful resident cook brought our evenings alive with nightly cookery lessons.

The food in the desert is much simpler than that found in the cities. We particularly liked a dish of vegetables cooked almost like a soup and served with lots of fluffy couscous to soak up the sauce. The vegetables were kept whole and simmered until really soft, while the couscous was steamed for two hours over a huge pot. However, we have devised a much quicker way of making it, given in this recipe.

The view on to the lake
at Ouarzazate

To serve, season the vegetables and pour them into a colourful bowl, or a tajine if you are lucky enough to possess one. Garnish with chopped parsley. Stir the butter into the hot couscous, then pile on a large flat plate or bowl. Shape into a mound and sprinkle with the toasted flaked almonds and cinnamon. If you like spicy food, this is delicious served with harissa (page 22) to give it a kick.

PRESERVED LEMONS

MAKES ABOUT 1 LITRE/1¾ PINTS

    450 g/1 lb lemons (4–6), plus juice   60 g/2 oz salt
       of about 4 more lemons

Cut the lemons into quarters, and cover the cut surfaces with salt. Put the lemons in a shallow bowl and cover with a weighted plate to help release juices. Leave for about 30 minutes.

Put the lemons and any juices that have collected in the bowl into a sterilized jar, pour on more lemon juice to moisten the lemons and just cover them, then seal. The preserved lemons can be used after about 3 weeks.

Alternatively, a quicker way is simply to cut lemons into quarters and blanch them in boiling water for 1 minute, then refresh them in cold water. This method isn't quite as authentic, but allows you to have almost the real thing in minutes, and you can do just enough for Ouarzazate Couscous (page 20)!

HARISSA

MAKES ABOUT 175 ML/6 FL OZ

    60 g/2 oz dried hot red chillies   4 garlic cloves
    2 tablespoons cumin seeds   1 teaspoon salt
    3 tablespoons coriander seeds   5 tablespoons olive oil

Remove the stems and seeds from the chillies, discard them and soak the chillies in warm water until soft, about an hour.

Grind the cumin and coriander seeds finely (if you wish you can toast them first briefly in a dry frying pan for more flavour).

Put the ground spices, drained soaked chillies, garlic and salt in a food processor and mix to a stiff paste. With the machine still running, slowly add the olive oil through the feeder tube until the paste becomes smooth.

A kasbah at Skoura oasis in the Dades valley
Inset **Preserved Lemons**

Preserved lemons are an ingredient in many Moroccan dishes, and harissa is used as a condiment all over the Maghreb. Both are easy to make and keep well in airtight jars in the fridge.

TOMATO AND CINNAMON CHUTNEY

MAKES ABOUT 125 ML/4 FL OZ

    5 tomatoes
    1 tablespoon brown sugar
    2 cinnamon sticks, ground

Blend all the ingredients together in a food processor, chill for about 1 hour and serve.

This very special, rather unusual chutney was served to us with a vegetable tajine in the heart of the medina in Marrakesh. Our hostess told us that many of her guests found it too strange, but she loved it — and so did I, although I am generally not a big fan of tomatoes.

CHERMOULA

SERVES 4–6

5 tablespoons olive oil	5 small courgettes, quartered
2 red onions, thinly sliced	lengthwise
3 garlic cloves, crushed	225 g/8 oz shelled fresh peas
2 teaspoons ground cumin	225 g/8 oz shelled fresh broad
1 teaspoon paprika	beans
½ scant teaspoon cayenne pepper	large handful of coriander leaves and
6 smallish potatoes, cut into	stems, chopped
quarters	juice of 1 lemon
450 g/1 lb tomatoes, puréed in a	salt and pepper
food processor	fresh hot baguette, to serve

Heat the oil in a large heavy-based saucepan. When it is hot, fry the onion until translucent. Then add the garlic and spices. Stir to keep them from sticking.

Add the potatoes and turn to coat them in the spices, then fry for 5 minutes. Add 225 ml/8 fl oz water and the puréed tomatoes. Bring to the boil and cook briskly until the sauce has reduced to a thick rich consistency with the oil returning on the top, adding the courgettes halfway through.

Add the peas, the broad beans and the chopped coriander, cover with a lid and simmer until all vegetables are soft. You may need to add a little more water to loosen the sauce and prevent sticking.

Finally pour in the lemon juice and add salt and pepper to taste. Serve with lots of fresh hot baguette.

We ate this dish when our car broke down near the fishing port of Essaouira and we were waiting for the fan belt to be fixed. Everyone was incredibly helpful and we had four mechanics on the job.

Chermoula is traditionally a fish dish and always includes a mixture of cumin, paprika, cayenne and lots of fresh coriander. If you do eat fish, simply fry fillets of white fish until they are crunchy and add to the mixture at the end of cooking. If fresh peas and broad beans are not available, frozen are the best option.

CARROT SALAD

Serves 4–6

350 g/12 oz carrots
salt and pepper
1 red onion
2 garlic cloves, crushed
2 tablespoons olive oil, plus more
    for sprinkling

½ teaspoon ground turmeric
½ teaspoon ground cumin
juice of 1 lemon
lots of flat-leaf parsley, chopped,
    to garnish

Peel the carrots and slice them thickly. Cook them in boiling salted water until soft.

Meanwhile, cut the red onion in half, then slice the halves thinly. Fry the sliced onions and the garlic in 2 tablespoons of the olive oil until soft. Stir in the turmeric and cumin.

Drain the carrots and refresh with cold water. Place in a serving bowl and add the cooked onion, garlic and spice mixture, with a good sprinkling of olive oil and the lemon juice. Season to taste and mix well.

Garnish with lots of flat-leaf parsley. Allow an hour for the flavours to penetrate the carrots before serving.

MOROCCAN MIXED SALAD PLATE

In Morocco, a salad of cucumber, tomato, red onion and olives is served with almost everything, so here is a suggested mixed plate. When buying tomatoes, it is always worth choosing plump beef tomatoes, or tomatoes on the vine, for a fuller flavour.

On a large plate, arrange slices of peeled cucumber, chunks of tomato, thin slices of red onion, and black and green olives. Then smother them in olive oil, lemon juice, black pepper and chopped fresh mint.

EGYPT, JORDAN & THE LEVANT

In this chapter any of the recipes given may be eaten together in any combination: the best thing to do is to mix and match the dishes as desired, including roast pitta bread with every meal. Bread plays an essential part in the diet of this region. Its Arabic name, *aysh*, means 'life', and it is part of every meal, from the most basic street snack to the grandest Bedouin feast. All the breads of the region are unleavened; the most well-known, pitta, is widely available in Europe and the US and is an ideal accompaniment to all these dishes; it is especially good for serving falafel in.

When we sailed down the Nile between Aswan and Luxor we had to take enough food for five days. With no means of refrigeration in the scorching desert heat our fresh supplies soon diminished, and the copious amount of fresh bread our boatman-cook had included became completely stale. However, simply by sprinkling the dry loaves with Nile water and tossing them over the coals of our fire he was able to provide us with bread that seemed as delicious as if it had just been baked — although there may well be something about cooking and eating under the stars on the bank of a great river, after a day's sailing through dramatic desert landscapes, that makes even simple food taste delicious.

In the souks of Cairo, Amman and Damascus we saw lavish displays of healthy vegetables piled high, but found the extent of vegetarian café food to be limited — although there were occasional surprises, such as the wonderful rocket salad encountered in Aqabah (see page 33). From Aqabah we visited Wadi Rum, where *Lawrence of Arabia* was filmed. While the desert landscape was every bit as dramatic as it had been on film, we were slightly disappointed to find coach parties arriving for 'Bedu tent suppers'. At Petra, however, we had no such disappointment. Riding on horseback through the narrow entrance to the gorge to come upon the majestic ruins of the ancient rose-red city was a dream achieved. We spent three days exploring Petra, the highlight of our trip to Jordan.

The last tribes of Bedouin living in the Badia Desert of eastern Jordan maintain a passion for the traditional desert style of eating mutton known as *mensaf*. This dish is a vegetarian's nightmare: a freshly slaughtered sheep is served on a bed of rice soaked in fat from the cooking; delicacies such as the tongue and eyes are offered to guests with great insistence. I spent several weeks visiting the Bedouin in their tents while photographing their way of life for the Royal Geographical Society, and when I was introduced as a vegetarian they went out of their way to provide me with alternatives.

Early-morning riders at the pyramids at Giza

The Bedouin are warm, hospitable, generous and entertaining hosts. The harsh desert environment has inspired traditions of providing food, drink and shelter to any passing stranger. The extreme heat of the day makes any exertion undesirable, and the shade and ventilation achieved by the design of their tents create an ideal environment in which to sit around on cushions and camel saddles escaping the unforgivng sun and indulging in long, relaxing tea-drinking ceremonies. Relatively few Bedouin still live as nomads, as falling water levels and competition for land increasingly threaten their future, and I felt very privileged to have spent some time, however brief, living among some of the last of them.

FUL MEDAMES

SERVES 4—6

3 teaspoons cumin seeds

8 tablespoons olive oil

5 garlic cloves, crushed

350 g / 12 oz dried fava or broad
   beans, soaked overnight

juice of 2 large lemons

large handful of flat-leaf parsley,
   chopped; more to garnish

salt and pepper

paprika, to garnish

2 lemons cut into wedges, to serve

For the Rocket and Grated Carrot Salad

2 handfuls of rocket

3 carrots, grated

lemon juice to taste

salt and pepper

For the Tomato and Cucumber Salad

4 large ripe tomatoes, diced

1 large cucumber, diced

1 red onion, cut into thin slices

4 sprigs of mint, chopped

lemon juice to taste

For the Beetroot Salad

3 cooked beetroots (with no added
   vinegar), diced

1 bunch of radishes, diced

2 red peppers, cut into cubes

handful of parsley, chopped

2 tablespoons olive oil

juice of 1 lemon

Dry-roast the cumin seeds in a small heavy pan until they are aromatic, then grind them to a powder.

In a large saucepan, heat 3 tablespoons of the olive oil. When hot, fry the garlic until soft. Add 2 teaspoons of the ground cumin and stir for a few seconds. Add the drained fava beans and stir until they are coated with oil.

Add enough water to cover the beans, bring to the boil, then simmer until the beans are nice and soft, for about an hour. You may need to add more water during this time to keep the beans moist and soupy.

Stir in the lemon juice, the remaining cumin and olive oil, the parsley, and salt and pepper to taste. As you stir, mash the beans so they start to break down.

Pile into a large bowl and sprinkle with paprika and chopped parsley to garnish. Place lemon wedges around the edge of the bowl. Make the three salads by simply combining the ingredients for each and serve with the ful medames.

Ful medames is served right across Egypt and Jordan, by everyone from street vendors and small cafés to the smartest hotels. It was our main dish on the last days of our boat journey down the Nile, and just the smell of the beans cooking brings back memories of our moonlit desert picnics.

We serve a slightly more sophisticated version of ful medames in the café, accompanied by fresh salads of beetroot, radishes, red onion, tomato, cucumber, carrot, plenty of parsley and coriander leaves, and of course roasted pitta bread. Traditionally, the dish should be very garlicky and smothered in olive oil and spices. You can even serve the beans for breakfast, with fried eggs and slices of ripe tomato.

Clockwise from top left
**Tabbouleh (page 31),
Jordanian Rocket Salad
(page 33) and Ful
Medames**

Above The Rose Tomb at Petra, cut out of marbled sandstone rocks
Right The entrance to the siq (gorge) at Petra, revealing the ancient pillars of the Khazneh (Treasury), one of the city's finest ruins

TABBOULEH

This is a beautiful speckled green salad from the mountains of Lebanon. We serve it with Falafel (page 32) and Hummus (page 35) or as part of a meze, a mixed salad plate.

SERVES 4–6

175 g/6 oz fine cracked bulghur wheat

6 medium tomatoes, finely diced

1 small cucumber, finely diced

4 tablespoons olive oil

juice of 2 lemons

salt and pepper

4 spring onions, thinly sliced, to garnish

lemon wedges, to serve

Soak the bulghur wheat in enough cold water to cover by 5 mm/¼ inch and leave for 15 minutes. The bulghur will double in size and should be light and fluffy when broken up with a fork or the fingers. If you have added too much water you can simply pour off the excess.

Add all the remaining ingredients and mix well. Garnish with spring onions and serve with lemon wedges.

VARIATION

If you would like to serve tabbouleh with the less traditional dressing that we use at the World Food Café, try the recipe below.

1 level dessertspoon grainy mustard

½ teaspoon sweet paprika

1 teaspoon honey

juice of 1 lemon

1 tablespoon cider vinegar

4 tablespoons olive oil

Mix the mustard, paprika and honey until you have a smooth paste, then slowly add the lemon juice, vinegar and olive oil. Stir into the mixture of bulghur wheat, tomatoes and cucumber.

Serve garnished with spring onions and lemon wedges.

FALAFEL

We serve these deep-fried balls of spiced mashed chickpeas in pitta bread with Tabbouleh (page 31), Hummus (page 35), lettuce and a salad of grated carrots. As the falafel are a little fiddly to make, we advise making them in big batches and keeping them in the freezer, so they're always there and all you have to do is fry them. They also make great party food.

SERVES 4–6

225 g/8 oz chickpeas, soaked
    overnight and cooked until soft
2 pitta breads or 2 slices of dry
    bread
1 large onion, coarsely chopped
2 garlic cloves
2 dessertspoons ground cumin
1 teaspoon ground chilli
2 dessertspoons plain flour
1 teaspoon salt
handful of flat-leaf parsley, chopped
sesame seeds, for coating
oil for frying, preferably sunflower

Chickpeas are quite tough, so blend them in 2 batches if you think your food processor isn't powerful or big enough.

Reduce the bread to crumbs in the processor. Add the onion, garlic, cumin, chilli, flour, salt and parsley, and blend to a paste.

With the machine still running slowly, add the chickpeas, until a thick paste forms. The consistency of this paste can vary slightly, depending on the moisture in the onion: if the mixture is too wet, simply make more breadcrumbs and combine; if too dry, add a small amount of water while blending.

Roll the mixture between your hands into 2.5 cm/1 inch balls and coat with sesame seeds. Fry the balls in hot oil until they are golden brown and crunchy.

If you are freezing the falafel, place cling-film between layers to make them easier to separate.

Falafel are served sizzling on pavements and in street cafés everywhere. In poorer rural areas they may share the pitta with little more than some dubious-looking limp salad (best declined) and a watery tahina (a creamed sesame paste with olive oil, garlic and lemon). In the bustling souks (markets) of Cairo, Amman and Damascus succulent concoctions of pickled vegetables, peppers, juicy tomatoes, crisp lettuce, yoghurt and thick creamy tahina are all crammed into the pitta along with the falafel balls to provide a whole meal on the hoof.

In restaurants falafel may be served on a side plate along with assorted dips such as baba ganoush (opposite) and various salads.

During a bargaining session for a Bedouin carpet in Aqabah, Jordan, we broke for lunch in a tiny backstreet café. Among other dishes, we were impressed to be served a huge plate of fresh rocket leaves with finely sliced red onion, olive oil and lemons.

This simple yet delicious meal put us in such a good mood that we settled the carpet deal somewhat in favour of the seller. Unfortunately, the carpet's vivid colours, so exciting in the Aqabah souk, had less appeal back in London. The carpet is long since forgotten in the attic, but we still remember the rocket salad.

JORDANIAN ROCKET SALAD

SERVES 4–6

3 large handfuls of rocket

handful of flat-leaf parsley, left on the stalk

4 tomatoes, diced

2 red onions, cut in half then thinly sliced

bunch of radishes, sliced

2 tablespoons olive oil

juice of ½ lemon

good pinch of ground cumin

salt and pepper

Mix the rocket and parsley. Make a bed of this in a salad bowl. On top of it, pile the tomato, onion and radishes.

Make a dressing with the olive oil, lemon juice, cumin, and salt and pepper to taste. Pour this over the salad and serve immediately.

BABA GANOUSH

This aubergine dip is good served with warm pitta bread.

SERVES 4–6

1 large aubergine

2 garlic cloves

2 tablespoons tahina

1 tablespoon olive oil

salt and pepper

juice of 1 lemon

chopped flat-leaf parsley, to garnish

paprika, to garnish

Grill the aubergine until the skin starts to bubble, turning it regularly until all sides are done and the aubergine feels soft. (This can also be done in a hot oven.)

Halve the aubergine and scoop out the flesh into a food processor. Add the garlic, tahina, olive oil, salt and pepper to taste and lemon juice, then blend until smooth.

Pile on a flat plate, garnish with parsley and sprinkle with paprika.

LENTIL SOUP

Serves 4–6

3 tablespoons olive oil

2 large onions, finely chopped

3 garlic cloves, crushed

350 g/12 oz red lentils

1.25 litres/2 pints stock

1½ teaspoons cumin seeds

1½ teaspoons crushed dried red
chillies

salt and pepper

juice of 1 lemon

handful of flat-leaf parsley, chopped

Rinse the lentils until the water runs clear. Heat the oil in a large heavy-based saucepan and fry the onions until soft. Add the garlic and fry for a few seconds.

Add the lentils to the pan and stir well until coated with oil. Add the stock and bring to the boil. If foam rises to the top, simply scoop off and discard.

Dry-roast the cumin seeds in a small pan until aromatic and then grind to a powder. Add this to the soup with the chilli flakes. Simmer with the lid on until the lentils are really soft and start to break down. You may need to add water during this time as lentils absorb a lot of liquid during cooking.

Add salt to taste, lots of freshly ground black pepper and lemon juice. Finally blend in a processor until smooth. Garnish with lots of freshly chopped parsley.

WHITE BEAN SALAD

Serves 4–6

425 g/15 oz canned butter beans

6 spring onions, sliced

2 garlic cloves, crushed

2 medium tomatoes, diced

1 small cucumber, peeled and finely
diced

1 green pepper, deseeded and finely
diced

handful of flat-leaf parsley, chopped

4 sprigs of mint, chopped

salt and pepper

juice of 1 lemon

2 tablespoons olive oil

black olives, to garnish

Drain the beans and combine them with all remaining ingredients. Serve garnished with black olives.

The lips of a statue at
Luxor dating from
4,000 years ago

HUMMUS

Serves 4–6

200 g/7 oz chickpeas, soaked
   overnight in plenty of water
2 garlic cloves
juice of 1½ lemons

3 tablespoons olive oil, plus more to
   dress
3 tablespoons tahina
ground cumin, to garnish

Drain the chickpeas and cook them in plenty of simmering water until soft.
Squash them between your fingers to see if they are done. Drain and allow
to cool.

Chickpeas are quite tough to blend, so do this in 2 batches if you have a
small processor. Put the chickpeas, garlic, lemon juice, oil and tahina in a
processor and blend until a thick paste forms. Now add a little water, bit by bit,
until the hummus becomes smooth and creamy. Season with salt to taste. Turn
out into a bowl and sprinkle with ground cumin, then drizzle with olive oil.

TURKEY

Despite the extent and centuries-long duration of the Ottoman Empire, the Turks did not trade extensively with other nations nor really receive an influx of foreign populations or cuisines. However, Turkish cooking uses many ingredients common also to the cuisines of Greece to the west and the Arab countries to the south-east.

One of our favourite meals in Turkey is breakfast. Warm fresh bread with local honey and butter, salty black olives, white sheep's-milk cheese and lots of refreshing tea is the standard hotel breakfast from Istanbul to the seaside villages of the Aegean. I ate my most memorable breakfast one day when I was the only passenger out on the deck of a ferry on a winter crossing of the Sea of Marmara. It was a bitterly cold morning, but the sight of the mosques of Istanbul appearing in the distance through the sea mist was well worth braving the cold for — especially as breakfast was served with a winter speciality of hot sweetened milk flavoured with orchid-root and cinnamon.

Chillies and lemons hanging up for sale on the Mediterranean coast of Turkey

IMAM'S AUBERGINE

SERVES 4–6

5 tablespoons olive oil

2 aubergines, diced

salt and pepper

275 g/10 oz white cabbage, thinly
sliced

1 dessertspoon paprika

400 g/14 oz creamed tomatoes
(thick, smooth sieved tomatoes

available from good
supermarkets) or passata, or 6
medium tomatoes puréed

large handful of flat-leaf parsley,
chopped

6 sprigs of mint, finely chopped

juice of 1 lemon

1 tablespoon honey or brown sugar

Heat the oil in a large saucepan. When hot, add the aubergine and sprinkle with a little salt to prevent the aubergine absorbing all the oil and drying out. When the aubergine starts to soften, add the cabbage. Continue frying until both vegetables are soft. Add the paprika and stir until the vegetables are coated.

Add the tomatoes and a little water to make a sauce, bring to the boil and simmer until the oil returns on top and the sauce looks nice and rich. You may need to add a little more water to prevent sticking.

Finally, add the parsley, mint, lemon juice, honey or sugar, and salt and pepper to taste. Cook for a further 5 minutes to allow all flavours to combine.

Serve with Mashed Carrot Salad (page 39), black olives, yoghurt and cucumber, and pitta bread, or with Tabbouleh (page 31) and Hummus (page 35).

The main component of the Turkish meze (mixed plate) that we serve in the World Food Café is this dish of aubergine and cabbage cooked in a herb and tomato sauce. We have come across similar dishes in Greek and Syrian cooking, usually known as 'the imam swooned', after a tale of an imam (Muslim prayer leader) who was so impressed with the taste that he fainted. We're not sure where the story or the recipe is originally from, so as we ate it first in Turkey we have included it here.

The rest of our meze is collected from all over the Middle East, including a mashed carrot salad, tabbouleh, hummus and olives.

TOMATO, CUCUMBER AND GREEN PEPPER

This works well in any Turkish meze. We ate it for breakfast, lunch and supper.

SERVES 4–6

4 ripe tomatoes, cubed

1 cucumber, cubed

2 green peppers, deseeded and
cubed

olive oil

pepper

Simply combine all ingredients with olive oil and black pepper to taste.

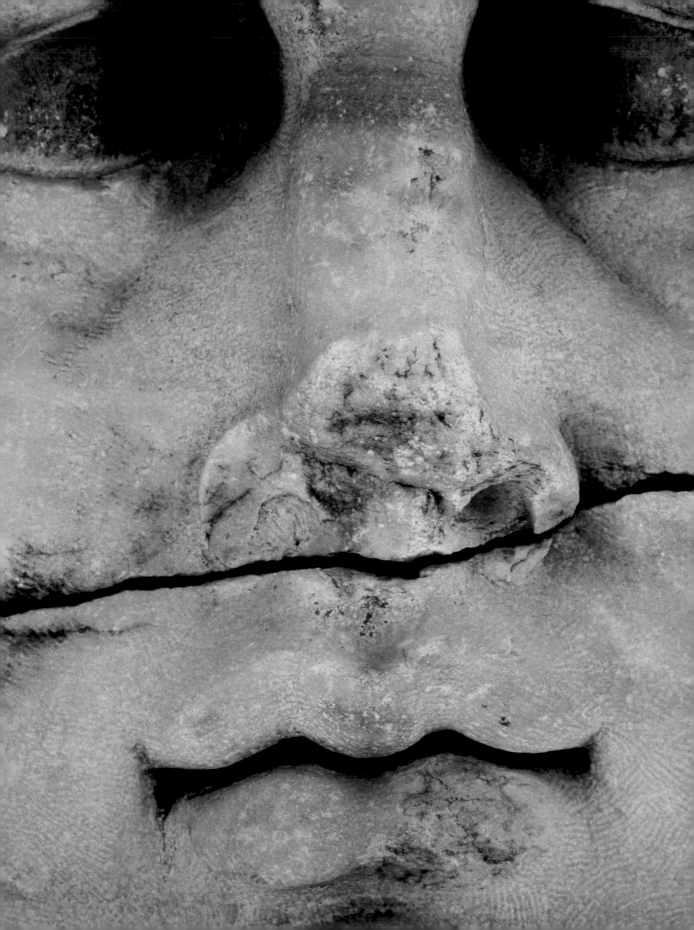

MASHED CARROT SALAD

This recipe is also delicious with yoghurt stirred into it.

SERVES 4–6

500 g / 1 lb 2 oz carrots, peeled and
    sliced
salt
1 level dessertspoon cumin seeds

juice of 1 lemon
3 tablespoons olive oil
1 teaspoon ground black pepper
1 level dessertspoon sweet paprika

Cook the carrots in boiling salted water until soft. Drain and place in a large bowl, then mash with a potato masher until smooth.

Dry-roast the cumin seeds in a small pan, then grind to a powder. Add to the mashed carrot with the remaining ingredients and mix well.

YOGHURT WITH CUCUMBER

This makes a very popular side-dish with any meal.

SERVES 4–6

1 cucumber, peeled and finely diced
300 ml / ½ pint yoghurt, preferably
    sheep's-milk

4 sprigs of mint, chopped
salt and pepper
1 tablespoon olive oil

In a bowl, combine all ingredients except the olive oil. Just before serving, pour the oil over the top of the salad.

A detail of the cracked face of a statue in the ruins at Didyma, an ancient sanctuary and oracle of Apollo

OMAN

In Oman, where meat is the customary offering to guests, the most interesting regional vegetarian dishes we found were in the road-house truckstops on the desert highway that stretches for a thousand kilometres across the 'empty quarter', linking the capital, Muscat, with Salalah, capital of the southern Dhofar region. These highway rest-stops are typical of the extreme contrasts in Oman. They are as clean and modern as if they were in Muscat, yet located in the heart of one of the most rugged and empty parts of the globe. Just inland from the gleaming high-tech cityscapes of Muscat, the Jebel Akhdar is a mountainous region of dirt roads and ancient villages, inhabited by turbanned men and veiled women. Age-old traditions of hospitality are still observed and we often found ourselves guests in people's homes, consuming dates and cardamom coffee.

Salalah is in many ways the most modern city in Oman; investment has been encouraged by the government. It is also a historic centre of the frankincense trade, on the edge of Dhofar, a wild land of warring tribes, remote mosques and desolate coastline. One fairly new development has been the establishment of a dairy industry, and in pastures recalling rural England, imported Friesian cattle graze alongside camels nibbling frankincense trees – another of the wonderful juxtapositions of modern Oman.

ROSEWATER RICE

SERVES 4–6

30 g / 1 oz butter
60 g / 2 oz raw shelled whole
  pistachio nuts
125 g / 4 oz raw almonds
125 g / 4 oz seedless raisins
30 g / 1 oz quartered dried apricots

450 g / 1 lb rice
½ teaspoon ground cardamom seeds
4 teaspoons rosewater
grated zest of 1 orange, preferably
  organic

Melt the butter in a large pan and fry the nuts until they brown. Add the raisins and apricots and keep warm on a very low heat.

Cook the rice in a large pan of simmering salted water until it is just tender. Drain well and sprinkle with the cardamom.

Add the nuts and fruit, sprinkle with rosewater and orange zest, and serve.

It may have been partly our relief at finding civilization in the wilderness, or perhaps the temptation of an unlimited buffet, but one way or another gluttony was an easy sin at the highway rest-stops in Oman. Bowls of aubergines in puréed date and yoghurt sauce, and mounds of rosewater rice are two of the delicious vegetarian dishes we found.

The Jebel Akhdar
Mountains

AUBERGINE IN A PURÉED DATE SAUCE

SERVES 4–6

4 tablespoons oil
3 medium red onions, thinly sliced
450 g / 1 lb aubergine, cubed
salt
1 teaspoon ground cinnamon
½ teaspoon ground ginger

¼ teaspoon ground allspice
250 ml / 9 fl oz stock
150 g / 5 oz dried dates
juice of 1 lemon
1 tablespoon rosewater

In a large pan, heat the oil. When hot, fry the onions until they are soft. Add
the aubergine and sprinkle it with a little salt to prevent it from absorbing
all the oil and drying out. Fry, stirring constantly, until the aubergine is
browned. Add the spices and fry for 1 minute. Add the stock and simmer
slowly for about 10 minutes.

In a food processor, purée the dates with the lemon juice and rosewater,
adding enough water to make a creamy paste. Add this paste to the aubergine,
stir in and serve.

MALI

The countries of French-speaking West Africa have inherited many food customs from their colonial past. Croissants, baguettes and *café au lait* are ubiquitous in restaurants and cafés — even in Bamako, capital of Mali, one of West Africa's poorest and least developed states. However, the street food, cooked and served outdoors, belongs to quite another tradition: the ingredients and style are wholly African.

The highlight of our trip to Mali was the annual migration of Fulani cattle across the Niger at the island village of Diafarabe (pages 10–11). Getting there took days of hard travel. We arrived at night to find a crowded village with no electricity; dawn revealed mud houses and a mosque among palm trees; fishermen casting nets into the Niger; and hundreds of cooking-fires filling the air with the smells of African breakfast. The herdsmen and cattle had been away in the Sahel for months, and their return was cause for celebration. Wives and families gathered on the river bank dressed in all their finery, as the Fulani chiefs, mounted on decorated horses and camels, galloped out of the desert in clouds of dust, then rode into the river, followed by thousands of long-horned cattle. The crossing continued long into the night, by which time Diafarabe was alive with music amplified with megaphones powered by truck batteries and dancing lit by hand torches.

WEST AFRICAN BEANS AND OKRA

SERVES 4–6

4 tablespoons oil	300 g / 10 oz green beans
1 onion, puréed	4 tomatoes, puréed in a food
1 teaspoon cayenne pepper	processor
1 tablespoon fresh thyme, chopped	handful of coriander leaves, chopped
18 medium-sized okra, cut in half	450 g / 1 lb cooked black-eyed beans
lengthwise	salt and pepper

Heat the oil in a large pan and, when hot, fry the onion until soft, then add the cayenne and thyme, and cook briefly. Add the okra, green beans, tomatoes and coriander, and cook on a low heat for 15 minutes, stirring occasionally.

Add the cooked black-eyed beans, mashing them a little with a fork. Season to taste with salt and pepper and add a little water to loosen the mixture. Serve.

This is a typical West African dish using okra, one of the most common vegetables of the region. We ate it at the weekly market in Djenné, near the mighty 15th-century mud-built mosque (page 13). The market brought to life the dusty square in front of the mosque and the sleepy alleys; people poured in from the countryside, and food-stalls appeared all around the square.

Jollof is a style of eating rice that usually includes meat and makes a meal in itself. This recipe is designed to cook rice in a similar way, but without meat. It makes a good accompaniment to the bean and okra dish opposite, or to Sweet Potatoes in a Cayenne, Ginger and Groundnut Sauce (page 44).

Pirogues – traditional canoes – on the Niger River

WEST AFRICAN JOLLOF RICE

SERVES 4–6

45 g/1½ oz butter
2 large onions, thinly sliced
2 large green peppers, deseeded and diced
1 teaspoon cayenne pepper
1 teaspoon ground black pepper

½ teaspoon ground allspice
225 g/8 oz tomatoes, finely chopped
125 g/4 oz tomato purée
1 tablespoon fresh chopped thyme
450 g/1 lb rice, rinsed
salt

Heat the butter in a large saucepan and fry the onions, green peppers and spices over a high heat for 1 minute. Add the tomatoes and fry for another minute. Stir in the tomato purée and the thyme and fry for 1 more minute. Add the rice, mix well and add enough water to cover the rice by about 1 cm/½ inch. Cover and bring to the boil. Reduce the heat and simmer until all the water is absorbed, about 15 minutes. Season with salt to taste and serve.

SWEET POTATOES IN A CAYENNE, GINGER AND GROUNDNUT SAUCE

SERVES 4–6

4 tablespoons sunflower oil

1 large onion, cubed

4 garlic cloves, crushed

5 cm/2 inch piece of root ginger, peeled and finely chopped

750 g/1¼ lb sweet potatoes, cubed

450 g/1 lb white cabbage, cubed

1 dessertspoon paprika

1 teaspoon cayenne pepper

400 g/14 oz chopped plum tomatoes (fresh or canned)

300 ml/½ pint pineapple juice

125 g/4 oz smooth peanut butter

salt and pepper

For the garnish

2 medium carrots, grated

2 medium raw beetroots, grated

2 bananas, sliced

juice of 1 lime

handful of coriander, chopped

Heat the sunflower oil in a large heavy pan. When hot, fry the onion until soft. Add the garlic and ginger, fry for a few minutes, then add the sweet potato and cabbage.

When the vegetables start to soften, add the paprika and cayenne pepper. Stir to coat the vegetables with the spices. Add the chopped tomatoes and pineapple juice. Cover the pan and simmer until the vegetables are soft.

Stir in the peanut butter until well combined. Season to taste.

Toss the carrot, beetroot and banana garnish in the lime juice and sprinkle over the dish, together with the coriander. Serve with rice.

This spicy sweet potato recipe is our all-time favourite West African dish, and one of our best memories of Mali. We tasted it on a riverboat journey along the Niger. Rather than eat the foul meals in the ship's restaurant, several Malians came equipped with stoves, pots and hampers of ingredients, and subsidized their fares by selling hearty stews.

We serve our version every day in the World Food Café. Each time we try to take it off the menu we are obliged by popular demand to bring it back. The ground peanuts – groundnuts – make a creamy sauce, enlivened with the fresh ginger, garlic and cayenne.

Sweet Potatoes in a Cayenne, Ginger and Groundnut Sauce

EAST AFRICA

East Africa is no paradise for vegetarians. Except in the Indian curry-houses of the cities, meat or seafood dishes are the most likely choice in any café or street stall anywhere in Kenya or Tanzania. However, spectacular skies, dramatic landscapes, wild animals and beautiful coastlines help to compensate for the lack of good vegetarian food. The most interesting dishes we found were on the Kenyan island of Lamu and the Tanzanian island of Zanzibar.

Apart from Zanzibar my main experience of Tanzania was photographing a Royal Geographical Society project in the heart of the savannah lands of Mkomazi Game Reserve. The reserve had never been developed or promoted as an international

A Masai tribesman on the edge of the Rift Valley in Tanzania

attraction, and the scientists were living in a group of huts on an escarpment over-looking the grasslands and the Paree Mountains beyond, in the midst of an undis-turbed wilderness. On arrival I was allocated a Land Rover and a ranger with a gun, and was given the freedom of the reserve. This turned out to be a dream assignment, giving me unlimited opportunity to photograph the African bush and enjoy some thrilling encounters with truly wild animals.

My next job was to photograph an upmarket luxury safari in the Serengeti and Ngorongoro Crater parks, including dawn balloon rides, lavish catering and five-star accommodation. Having previously imagined that *this* would be the dream assign-ment, in practice I found the experience of being driven around the bush with a group much less exciting than that of being out on my own.

ZANZIBAR BEANS IN COCONUT SAUCE

For a more authentic version of this dish, fresh fish or seafood can be used instead of the sweet potatoes.

Zanzibar, politically part of Tanzania, owes its cooking traditions more to Arab and European colonialism and to Indian traders than to mainland East Africa. Coconut-palm groves and spice plantations provide ingredients for tasty sauces.

We rented a house with a cook on the quiet east coast. He was most enthusiastic about cooking us lobster, giant prawns and fish fillets in a rich coconut-cream sauce, but we did manage to get him to prepare the same sauce with beans and fried sweet potatoes, as given here, and it was just as good.

SERVES 4–6

6 tablespoons oil	4 cardamom pods, split
450 g / 1 lb sweet potatoes, cut into 2 cm / ¾ inch cubes	2 teaspoons ground turmeric
1 large onion, finely chopped	6 green chillies, cut into quarters lengthwise
6 garlic cloves, crushed	handful of fresh coriander leaves
5 cm / 2 inch piece of root ginger, peeled and chopped	400 ml / 14 fl oz canned coconut milk
4 black peppercorns, coarsely ground	450 g / 1 lb cooked beans (pinto, black-eyed or cow pea)
6 cloves, coarsely ground	salt

Heat half the oil in a heavy pan and, when hot, fry the sweet potato until almost cooked. Set aside.

In the remaining oil, fry the onion, garlic and ginger until soft. Add all the spices with the chillies and coriander, and cook, stirring, for 3 minutes.

Add the coconut milk, the sweet potato and the beans. Simmer gently until the sweet potato is quite tender. Season with salt to taste and serve.

BERBERÉ PASTE

In Ethiopia, berberé means red chilli powder, but it is also the spicy paste that makes Ethiopian food so distinctive. It can be made in advance and kept in the fridge for up to 6 weeks.

SERVES 4–6

2 garlic cloves	⅓ teaspoon fenugreek seeds
1 cm / ½ inch cube of root ginger, peeled and coarsely chopped	4 cloves
3 spring onions or ¼ medium onion, sliced	1 teaspoon cumin seeds
	7 dried red chillies
1 tablespoon vinegar	¼ teaspoon ground cinnamon
½ teaspoon black peppercorns	¼ teaspoon ground nutmeg
½ teaspoon cardamom seeds	1 teaspoon salt
½ teaspoon coriander seeds	4 teaspoons ground paprika
	¼ teaspoon ground allspice

In a food processor, blend the garlic, ginger, onion and vinegar until a paste forms.

Dry-roast the black peppercorns, cardamom seeds, coriander seeds, fenugreek seeds, cloves and cumin seeds in a hot frying pan until toasted. Add the chillies and grind the mixture finely in a spice grinder or using a pestle and mortar. Add to the paste.

Add the remaining ingredients and mix well. Store in a well-sealed container.

Ethiopia, in northern East Africa, can be a schizophrenic country for a vegetarian traveller. Ethiopians have a unique and interesting tradition of spicy stews, or wats (*w'ets*), based on lamb, goat or beef. However, many Ethiopians are Orthodox Christians required to 'fast' on Wednesdays and Fridays. 'Fasting' in this sense consists of eating wats without the meat – so a genuine retinue of tasty Ethiopian wats is made using vegetables, beans and lentils. During Lent in March and April there are several weeks of fasting, when vegetarians can feast daily without restriction.

The two recipes we give here are for berberé paste – the essential ingredient of a good wat – and for a wat made with mixed vegetables.

ETHIOPIAN VEGETABLE WAT

Any combination of vegetables can be used in this dish; the mixture used here is just a suggestion. In Ethiopia, the traditional accompaniment to this wat would be injera, a spongy, slightly fermented pancake-type of bread. In the café we serve it with cheese-and-herb bread, cottage cheese and salad.

SERVES 4–6

45 g/1½ oz butter

1 large onion, thinly sliced

2 garlic cloves, crushed

1 tablespoon berberé paste (see opposite)

1 teaspoon paprika

1 teaspoon ground turmeric

1 teaspoon ground cardamom seeds

1 clove, ground

7.5 cm/3 inch piece of cinnamon stick, ground

3 medium carrots, cubed

3 medium potatoes, cubed

3 courgettes, chopped into chunks

200 g/7 oz green beans, chopped

200 g/7 oz spring greens, chopped

400 g/14 oz canned chopped tomatoes

250 ml/9 fl oz stock

salt and pepper

6 fresh basil leaves, torn up

handful of fresh coriander leaves, chopped

Melt the butter in a large heavy pan and, when hot, fry the onion, garlic and berberé paste for 3 minutes. Add the spices and cook, stirring, for 2 minutes more. Add all the fresh vegetables and stir into the spices. Continue to cook for 10 minutes, stirring occasionally.

Add the tomatoes with their liquid and the stock, bring to the boil and simmer until the vegetables are all cooked, adding more water if needed. Season to taste with salt and pepper.

Finally, add the torn basil leaves and coriander.

MKOMAZI CARDAMOM-MASHED SWEET POTATO WITH PEPPER RELISH

This mash, served here with a zingy relish, would also be good with an onion gravy.

SERVES 4–6

250 g/9 oz sweet potatoes	*For the relish*
250 g/9 oz sweetcorn kernels	3 garlic cloves
175 g/6 oz shelled fresh peas	3 fresh red chillies
250 g/9 oz spinach	4 tomatoes
45 g/1½ oz butter	1 onion, chopped
1 large onion, sliced	1 large red pepper, deseeded and
1 teaspoon ground cardamom seeds	chopped
salt and pepper	handful of fresh parsley
1 teaspoon honey	juice of 1 lemon
	salt and pepper

Well ahead, make the relish: in a food processor, blend together all the ingredients with 2 tablespoons water and seasoning to taste. Set aside, preferably in the fridge, and leave as long as you can – the longer the better.

Cook the sweet potatoes in boiling salted water until they are soft enough to mash. Drain.

Cook the corn and peas in boiling salted water until tender. Just before the end of cooking, add the spinach to wilt it briefly. Drain.

Melt the butter in a heavy pan, then fry the onion in it until it is well caramelized.

Combine the sweet potatoes and the onion, sprinkle with cardamom, salt and pepper and mash, adding more butter if desired. Add the other vegetables and mix in the honey.

Serve hot, with the relish and a green salad.

During my stay on the Mkomazi Game Reserve in Tanzania, the camp cook noticed my lack of enthusiasm for his meat stews and offered to cook me something special if I drove him to the village for some ingredients. Gathering the ingredients took about half an hour; sitting around in the bar meeting all his friends over several beers took the rest of the afternoon.

After weeks of meat stews, the others in the camp were so interested in my superb meal that the cook found himself making it for everyone the following evening.

Mkomazi Cardamom-mashed Sweet Potato and (inset) Pepper Relish

CASSAVA AND CELERY IN MUNG DAL GRAVY

We were served this dish in a Nairobi home as a vegetarian alternative to the traditional meat sauces that accompany the maize-meal staple, ugali. We serve it with rice and salad instead of ugali. Cassava is not always easy to find (sometimes it is available frozen) and must be well cooked. Sweet potatoes make a perfectly acceptable alternative.

SERVES 4–6

250 g/9 oz mung dal
625 g/1 lb 6 oz cassava or sweet
   potato, cut into 2 cm/¾ inch
   cubes
4 tablespoons groundnut oil
2 large onions, finely chopped

1 teaspoon ground turmeric
1 teaspoon chilli powder
1 teaspoon paprika
1 head of celery, chopped small
salt

Cook the mung dal in boiling water until softish, drain and partially mash. Parboil the cassava in boiling salted water for about 10 minutes, drain and set aside.

Heat the oil in a large heavy pan. When hot, fry the onions until they are soft. Add the spices and fry for 1 minute more. Add the cassava and celery. Fry until the vegetables are tender, about 2–3 minutes.

Stir in the cooked dal, with salt to taste and enough water to give a sauce-like consistency.

Orphaned baby elephants in the Daphne Scheldrick Sanctuary of Nairobi Park

THE SEYCHELLES: LA DIGUE ISLAND

La Digue is one of the 115 islands of the Seychelles. With a population of around 2,000 it is a friendly and relaxed place, with all the trappings of a tropical paradise. There are abundant forests full of fruits; palm-fringed beaches of white sand and warm, clear water full of fish; and long days of sunshine and blue sky. We also discovered some wonderful food.

We stayed in an old French colonial plantation house converted into a guest-house, in which the evening meals provided by the family that own and run it were exceptional. The cooks were more than happy to let us sit in on their preparations and find out how they created the meals we were eating. The recipes we give in this chapter are two of our favourites.

La Digue was an uninhabited desert island until just over 200 years ago. It was first settled by French colonialists and their slaves, then gained by the British, along with most of the Indian Ocean islands, as spoils of the Napoleonic wars. With the abolition of slavery the British encouraged the migration of Indian and Oriental Asians to the islands. La Digue gradually developed as a community with the rich ethnic blend of African, Asian, Arab and European genes and cultural influences that define the Creole-speaking Seychellois and their food. The finest traditional cooking is probably found in the guest-houses, where meals are eaten communally as buffet feasts. Fresh fish and Creole sauces dominate, and there are also some delicious and inventive vegetable and salad accompaniments.

Much of the appeal of La Digue lies in the things it lacks – such as tropical diseases, crime, cars, poverty, pollution, large hotels, crowds, and dangerous wildlife. Being such an intimate island society, violent crime is virtually unheard of and even petty theft is extremely unlikely. Apart from the island's two taxis, vehicles are restricted to a few pickups used by the local farmers and traders, bicycles, and creaking ox-carts – which also operate as taxis.

The island is only 4 km (2.5 miles) long, and cycling is a pleasure on the shaded, carless roads which give access to most of the coast and the less mountainous parts of the interior. If you leave your bike, unlocked, at the end of a road and continue by foot, jungly tracks will take you to some of the most stunning beaches in the world.

One of the paradise beaches of La Digue island

SWEET APPLE SALAD

In the Seychelles Sweet Apple Salad is almost always served with Creole dishes. Golden apples – tart green apples rather like small Granny Smith's but with flesh that is drier and more yellow – are combined with bredes, a local variety of spinach which is in fact more like Chinese leaf. The resulting salad is a wonderful balance of sweet, savoury and spicy.

SERVES 4–6

4 tart apples, grated
½ medium head of Chinese leaf, thinly sliced
2 tablespoons sunflower oil
1 large red onion, cut in half and then thinly sliced

2 green chillies, thinly sliced
½ teaspoon ground turmeric
2.5 cm / 1 inch cube of root ginger, grated
juice of 2 limes
salt and pepper

Combine the grated apple and sliced Chinese leaf.

Heat the oil in a frying pan and fry the onion until it starts to soften. Add the chillies, turmeric and ginger and fry for a further 30 seconds.

Stir the contents of the pan into the salad, then sprinkle it with the lime juice and freshly ground black pepper. Add salt to taste and mix well.

Chill for half an hour before serving.

CARRI COCO CURRY

SERVES 4–6

125 g/4 oz butter

1 tablespoon sunflower oil

2 large onions, diced

5 garlic cloves, crushed

3.5 cm/1½ inch cube of root ginger, peeled and grated

2 medium sweet potatoes (preferably orange-fleshed), cut into cubes

4 carrots, cubed

1 butternut squash, peeled and cubed (about 500 g/1 lb 2 oz)

400 g/14 oz Chinese leaf, cut into 2.5 cm/1 inch strips

large handful of flat-leaf parsley, finely chopped

small handful of thyme, finely chopped

400 ml/14 fl oz coconut milk

salt and pepper

For the curry mixture

10 curry leaves

1 teaspoon ground cinnamon

½ teaspoon chilli powder

1 teaspoon ground allspice

¼ teaspoon cayenne pepper

1 teaspoon ground black pepper

1 teaspoon ground turmeric

For the garnish

2 plantains

2 tablespoons oil or 30 g/1 oz butter

Coco curry is traditionally made with coconut milk and herbs, and served with fish. Sweet potato, cassava and bread fruit form a large part of the Creole daily diet, so those are what we cook it with at the World Food Café. You can, however, make it with almost any vegetable. We have chosen sweet potato and butternut squash, which are more readily available.

Melt the butter in a large saucepan, without allowing it to burn. Add the oil. Fry the onion, garlic and ginger until soft. Add the curry mixture and stir.

Throw in the sweet potato, carrot and butternut squash. Stir until the vegetables are well coated with spice mix. Add just enough water barely to cover the vegetables. Bring to the boil, reduce the heat and simmer until the vegetables just start to soften.

Add the Chinese leaf, parsley, thyme and coconut milk. Cook gently for a further 10 minutes, making sure the coconut milk does not boil. Season with salt and pepper to taste.

While the curry is cooking, slice the plantain and fry the slices in hot oil until crunchy on the outside and soft inside. Sprinkle with salt.

Serve with rice, fried plantain slices and Sweet Apple Salad (page 55).

Sweet Apple Salad (front) and Carri Coco Curry (back)

India, Nepal &

Sri Lanka

India, Nepal & Sri Lanka

A plate of several Indian dishes, or thali, is a daily feature of the World Food Café menu. The many regional variations of Indian cooking provide a wide choice of cooking styles for the main dish, which is served with home-made chutneys, salads, raitas and rice. Indian cuisine displays an extensive range of vegetarian cooking, and the friendly hospitality of the people, their love of food and their eagerness to share how it is prepared have given us a great collection of recipes. Some of these we gathered without a word of common language in remote rural homes; others were demonstrated in fluent English in smart city apartments; still others were acquired in quite bizarre circumstances.

Travelling in India can be a confusing mix of sensuous experiences. During one trip there I read in a book the line 'like mustard gas and roses'. The phrase, for me, sums up travelling in India. Smells come as gross as mustard gas and as sweet as roses within seconds of each other. Sights are seductive, poetic and romantic as often as revolting, pitiful and disturbing. Travel can include many hours of boredom, discomfort and frustration and just as many of excitement, luxury and pleasure. Travelling anywhere has elements of all these aspects, but India manages to deliver more of them, more often, and more extremely.

All the domestic airlines have vegetarian food on board, while long rail journeys are made even more memorable by excellent vegetarian thalis delivered freshly cooked to your seat. Roadside cafes, or *dhabas*, where the long-distance buses stop, provide slap-up feasts for hundreds at a time. If you travel by hired car you will inevitably have a driver who knows the best *dhabas* and will be pleased to stop when you fancy a roadside meal. Some hotels have good buffets with many vegetarian options, although often a better meal can be found for a modest sum in a local café. There is no shortage of interesting vegetarian street food: on city streets, railway platforms and beaches, at bus stations, markets and even lonely road-junctions there are stalls churning out sizzling snacks.

We have divided India into north, east, south and west to reflect the areas where we discovered different dishes. There are far more complex regional variations than this in Indian cooking, and the mobility of the population means you can end up eating almost anything, anywhere. In general, the food of the south often includes coconut and is served with lots of rice, with lots of pickles, chutneys and small side-dishes. In the north there is a fondness for ghee (clarified butter) and paneer (fried cheese); the food can be rich and oily and is often served with breads to soak up the oil. Some dishes, such as aloo gobi, turn up all

Above **A snack seller in southern India displays his enticing wares.**
Right **Children in the Shekhawati district of Rajasthan. The pleasure of travel in India is as much to do with the beauty and sense of humour of the people as it is to do with seductive landscapes or remarkable buildings.**

Pages 58-59 **Crossing the bridge, Madurai, Tamil Nadu**

over India in various styles. In poorer rural areas the options may be as limited as dal, rice and samosas, while in cities the choice can be bewildering.

Nepal and Sri Lanka, both bordering India although thousands of kilometres apart, have cuisines influenced by the style of Indian cooking. Meals in Nepal are usually robust and filling, combinations of boiled rice, creamy dal and spiced vegetables, providing good fuel for long walks between mountain villages. The year-round tropical heat of Sri Lanka encourages lighter meals with an emphasis on coconuts, curry leaves and tangy mixtures of fresh fruit and fiery chillies.

In the World Food Café we serve the Indian thali with long-grain brown rice (preferring white basmati at home). The amount of chilli to use is a personal decision; the recipes here use the amount shown to us by the people who made the dishes. In the café we advise people who are sensitive to spicy food to avoid the Indian dishes, but most customers find it fine. If you reduce the quantity of chilli in any recipe you won't alter the overall flavour too much, so feel free to scale it down (or up) as your personal preference dictates.

NORTHERN INDIA

The far north of India has more in common with Tibet than it does with the rest of the subcontinent. The Himalayan peaks and snowfields of Ladakh form a backdrop to Buddhist monasteries and shrines; most of the people are Tibetan rather than Indian in origin, a fact reflected in the style of the food. The lake district of Kashmir is distinctive in a different way, owing more to the Islamic traditions of Central Asia than to the plains of India. Kashmiri-inspired dishes crop up all over the north. Sadly, since our last visit at the end of the 1980s, Kashmir has effectively been closed to casual tourism. We still have fond memories of home-cooked meals eaten on wooden houseboats on Dal Lake.

Water taxis like this elegant yellow *shikara* are used to ferry tourists and Kashmiris around Dal and Naki lakes.

Dal and rice form the staple diet across India. The recipe for dal fry given here is less refined than some in this chapter, yet the dish is utterly delicious.

Located in the foothills of the Himalayas along the flood-plain of the Ramganga River, the Corbet National Park is only few hours north of Delhi, yet it could not be a more serene and peaceful place. The first time we went there we had unrealistic expectations of seeing a wild tiger. The dawn and dusk elephant-rides through the forest, the sightings of deer, monkeys and other wildlife, the great natural beauty, and the fine evening meals in the forest lodge were all very enjoyable, but we still felt frustrated by the lack of tiger. When we left I filled in the visitors' book and was asked to list all the animals I had seen. I cheekily ended by writing 'BUT NO TIGER' — and was left looking slightly ridiculous when the bus to the park gates had to stop to wait for a fine, full-grown tigress and her cubs to stroll across the road and off into the jungle.

DAL FRY

Lentils are cooked until they form a creamy soup; the spices are fried and added at the end of the cooking. Serve the dal simply with rice or as an accompaniment to any curry.

SERVES 4–6

250 g/9 oz yellow split peas
5 cm/2 inch piece of root ginger, peeled and grated
½ teaspoon ground turmeric
2 tablespoons ghee or butter (or sunflower oil)

4 garlic cloves, thinly sliced
1 dessertspoon black mustard seeds
1 teaspoon cumin seeds
6 small red chillies
salt
chopped coriander leaves, to garnish

Rinse the yellow split peas until the water runs clear. Place in a saucepan and cover with 700 ml/1¼ pints water. Bring to the boil; a foam will rise to the top of the pan, simply scoop this off and discard.

Add the ginger and turmeric and simmer until the split peas become very soft and break up. The dal should be smooth and like a thick soup. Lentils do absorb a lot of water, so you may need to add more during the cooking time.

Melt the ghee in a small frying pan, add the garlic slices and fry until they are golden brown. Add the mustard seeds, cumin seeds and chillies; when they start to 'pop' (after just a few seconds), remove from heat and pour over the dal. Stand back slightly as it will crackle and spit.

Finally add salt to taste and garnish with chopped coriander leaves.

KASHMIRI GOBI

This is a northern Indian way of cooking cauliflower, using cashew nuts and cayenne pepper, together with an aromatic creamed tomato sauce. It makes a good main dish, along with Nalagarh Brinjal (page 66) and orange rice (page 67).

SERVES 4–6

1 large onion

4 garlic cloves

5 cm/2 inch piece of root ginger, peeled

3 medium tomatoes

6 tablespoons oil

1 large cauliflower, separated into florets

1 teaspoon ground turmeric

1 teaspoon cayenne pepper

1 teaspoon ground cinnamon

½ teaspoon ground cloves

1 teaspoon ground cardamom seeds

4 bay leaves

1 teaspoon sugar

1 teaspoon salt

For the garnish

30 g/1 oz cashew nuts, toasted

30 g/1 oz raisins

Purée the onion, garlic, ginger and tomatoes together in a food processor.

Heat the oil in a large heavy pan and, when hot, fry the cauliflower until it is beginning to brown and soften, then remove.

Fry the purée with the turmeric and cayenne for 3 minutes. Then add the cinnamon, cloves, cardamom, bay leaves, sugar and salt.

Return the cauliflower to the mixture and turn to coat well and heat through.

Serve garnished with the toasted cashew nuts and raisins.

Kashimiri Gobi, Nalagarh Brinjal and Narangi Pulao were among the many dishes we ate while photographing Nalagarh Fort, the ancestral home of the maharaja Vijayendra Singh, situated in the foothills of the Himalayas. We went there just before it was opened as a hotel; the cooks were old family retainers, and must by now be cooking some of these recipes for the hotel guests. Kashmiri Gobi is a recipe brought into the family by the Maharani, who came from the western side of Kashmir, which is now part of Pakistan.

Kashmiri Gobi

NALAGARH BRINJAL

This side-dish of aubergine in yoghurt is quite luxurious, as is appropriate for the table of a maharaja.

SERVES 4–6

1 large aubergine, cut into rounds
   1 cm/½ inch thick
1 teaspoon ground turmeric
salt
5 tablespoons sunflower oil
450 g/1 lb Greek-style yoghurt
125 ml/4 fl oz double cream

3 garlic cloves, crushed
2.5 cm/1 inch cube of root ginger,
   peeled and crushed
2 green chillies, finely chopped
handful of fresh coriander leaves,
   chopped, for garnish

Sprinkle the aubergine slices with the turmeric and some salt. Get the oil very hot in a frying pan and fry the aubergine slices, a few at a time, until well browned, then drain on kitchen paper.

In a food processor, blend the yoghurt, cream, garlic, ginger and chillies. Place the aubergine slices on a flat dish and pour over the mixture.

Serve garnished with coriander.

Above left **Narangi Pulao and Lassi (page 83)**
Above right **A man smokes a hookah at dusk on Dal Lake.**

Narangi pulao can be eaten as a side-dish with almost any curry or dal. The traditional way to serve it at Nalagarh is with a layer of fried potato-and-yoghurt mixture sandwiched between the rice, making it into a whole meal.

The dish is similar to the rice we ate in Oman (see page 40), cooked in an essentially Persian style: the similarity again reflects the historical family connections with lands farther to the west in the days before the partition of India.

NARANGI PULAO

SERVES 4–6

450 g/1 lb potatoes, cut into
    small cubes
4 tablespoons oil
1 onion, puréed
4 garlic cloves, puréed
3 cloves
3 cardamom pods, split
1 cinnamon stick, broken up
1 teaspoon cayenne pepper
4 bay leaves
250 g/9 oz full-fat yoghurt
juice of 1 lemon
rosewater

For the orange rice
3 oranges, preferably unwaxed
450 g/1 lb basmati rice, washed,
    soaked and drained
3 tablespoons oil
1 tablespoon sugar
2 onions, very thinly sliced
8 cloves
8 cardamom pods, split to release
    the seeds
salt
12 cashew nuts
12 whole almonds

To make the orange rice: peel the oranges and cut the rind into thin strips. Chop the oranges into cubes, discarding pips and pith. Put the rind with 6 cups of water, 1 tablespoon of oil and the sugar into a pan and boil for 5 minutes.

Meanwhile, fry the onion, cloves and cardamom seeds in the remaining oil until brown. Season with salt to taste, then add the drained rice. Stir to coat the rice, then add the orange rind with the boiling water. Cook until the rice is tender, about 12 minutes.

To serve as a side-dish, garnish with the cubes of orange and the cashews and almonds lightly fried in butter.

To make the main-course dish: fry the potatoes in half the oil until crispy and set aside. Fry the puréed onion and garlic in the remaining oil until brown. Add the cloves, cardamom, cinnamon, cayenne and bay leaves, and cook for a minute. Add the yoghurt and lemon juice, and cook slowly for 10 minutes, then stir in the potatoes.

To complete the dish, place half the rice on a flat dish, pour on the yoghurt and potato mixture, then put the other half of the rice on top.

Serve garnished with the fried almonds and cashews and the orange pieces as above, then sprinkle with a little rosewater.

POTATO BONDAS

These potato fritters are particularly good served with Green Coconut Chutney (page 84).

SERVES 4–6

oil for deep-frying

1 kg/2¼ lb potatoes, cooked and
  mashed

2 tablespoons sunflower oil

½ teaspoon salt

2 teaspoons sugar

4 teaspoons desiccated coconut

5–10 green chillies, finely chopped

2 pinches of hing (asafoetida)

5 cm/2 inch piece of root ginger,
  very finely chopped

1 teaspoon sesame seeds

1 teaspoon garam masala

juice of 1 lime

handful of coriander leaves, chopped

For the batter

6 tablespoons gram flour

pinch of salt

pinch of hing (asafoetida)

1 teaspoon ground turmeric

1 teaspoon chilli powder

Mix all the batter ingredients together in a bowl, adding a little water a spoonful at a time until a thick paste forms.

Heat the oil for deep-frying.

Mix all the rest of the ingredients together and mould by hand into balls about the size of a golf ball.

When the oil is hot enough to cause a drop of the batter to sizzle and bubble rapidly, dip each ball of mixture in the batter and deep-fry in 2–3 batches, turning regularly until golden brown all over, 5–10 minutes. Drain on kitchen paper and serve hot or cold.

For convenience, the balls may instead be flattened out a bit and shallow-fried, turning once.

Potato bondas make a wonderful snack or starter and keep for several days, so it's worth making quite a lot at a time. We made a whole tinful to take skiing in Kashmir, filling our ski-jacket pockets with them at the beginning of each day so that we could snack on them during ski-lift rides. As the balls are quite fragile they also provided an extra incentive not to fall over.

The bondas are supposed to be very spicy, so they are particularly good to eat on the cold snow slopes. When I offered one to a Scandinavian skier sharing my chair lift, he found it excessively hot and, as soon as we got off, grabbed mouthfuls of snow to relieve his burning mouth. This recipe has been considerably toned down to make a milder version – if you want to spice it up again just add more chilli.

Potato Bondas, with Green Coconut Chutney (page 84)

EASTERN INDIA

Eastern India attracts far fewer foreign tourists than the west. When we went to the annual Sonepur Elephant Mela (fair) on a tributary of the Ganges near Patna in Bihar, we were among only a small handful of foreigners. The Mela, along with a full-moon pilgrimage, attracts just as many revellers, traders and devotees as the Camel Mela does on the same night over in Rajasthan (see page 86), yet here nearly all of them are locals. There is plenty of interesting food available from the dozens of stalls. Also fascinating is the sight of so many elephants being manipulated between surging crowds of humanity. Occasionally an elephant breaks free, causing scenes of panic and great amusement, but most of the time they are occupied in eating or being washed, decorated or otherwise pampered, and maintain a regal air of disregard for all around them.

From Patna we travelled by train to Calcutta, sitting next to a man whose family owned a small hotel there (his card described it as 'located in posh area'). We decided to give it a go, and found the East West Guest House the perfect base from which to explore the extraordinary city. It was located not only in a pleasantly 'posh' area but also above a first-rate street café.

On our way back to Delhi we spent a few days in Varanasi, that most holy of Hindu cities, on the holiest river, the Ganges. We arrived at night and strolled along the riverbank beneath the towering walls of the old city, past series of steps, or ghats, leading to the water. Turning a corner we were confronted with a scene of medieval intensity. The walls were illuminated by golden light from roaring fires, crowds of wailing, hooded people blocked the way, men in loincloths scurried here and there, priests were chanting and ringing bells, and incense wafted about, together with a smell of burning flesh. The fires were funeral pyres: we had reached the burning-ghat of Manikamika.

We fell in love with Varanasi, and have returned several times — once during Divali, the Hindu Festival of Lights. The narrow alleyways and courtyards were lit by thousands of candles and butter lamps, and echoed to the sounds of temple singing and 'bottle bomb' fireworks. In the midst of the carnival-style festivities we watched four old men, seemingly oblivious to all the activity, carry a large dead cow down to the Ganges. They precariously floated it out into the river between two small boats, and silently let it sink into the current. They returned to the shore without exchanging a word, then slipped off separately into the shadows.

A ferry across the Ganges at Varanasi

CALCUTTA AUBERGINE

SERVES 4–6

1 large onion, chopped
12 garlic cloves
6 green chillies
6 tablespoons sunflower oil
3 teaspoons ground paprika
½ teaspoon cayenne pepper
1 teaspoon ground turmeric

450 g/1 lb baby aubergine, cut into
    quarters lengthwise
3 teaspoons tamarind purée
2 teaspoons finely chopped jaggery
    or brown sugar
handful of coriander leaves, chopped

Blend the onion, garlic and chillies in a food processor.

Heat the oil in a large heavy pan and, when hot, fry the mixture with the paprika, cayenne and turmeric for 3 minutes. Add the aubergine and cook for 5 minutes more. Dissolve the tamarind in a little water and stir in, then add the jaggery. Cook until the aubergines become soft.

Serve garnished with lots of fresh coriander, and accompanied by chapatis.

This is one of the dishes we ate regularly in Calcutta, sitting on low wooden benches under one of the huge shade-giving board trees on the pavement beneath our guest-house. The street café, operating out of a typically Calcuttan hole in the wall, had the added bonus of being so popular with taxi drivers that we could always be sure of a cab straight after our meal. The food was so good that we hardly ate anywhere else.

Above **The Calcuttan 'hole-in-the-wall' café**
Right **Calcutta Aubergine**

ORISSAN JAGDISH SAAG ALOO

Serves 4–6

6 tablespoons oil

2 tablespoons dried red chillies

2 teaspoons black mustard seeds

5 medium potatoes, cubed, soaked in cold water for a few hours, then drained well

2 tablespoons fresh fenugreek leaves

6 garlic cloves, crushed

1 thumb-sized piece of root ginger, peeled and finely chopped

3 green chillies, finely chopped

450 g / 1 lb fresh spinach, finely chopped

Heat the oil in a large heavy pan and, when hot, add the dried chillies, stirring to turn them in the oil. Add the mustard seeds and cook them briefly until they pop. Add the potatoes, a spoonful at a time so as not to lower the heat of the oil too much, and stir-fry for 5 minutes.

Add the fenugreek leaves, garlic, ginger and green chillies. Continue to stir-fry until the potatoes start to break up. Add the spinach and loosen with a little water. Serve when the spinach has wilted.

We rented a house for a few weeks on the coast of Orissa, in the eccentric village of Gopalpur-on-Sea. During our stay there, we passed several jovial evenings in the homes of local minor dignitaries, but most of our meals were enjoyed in the hub of Gopalpur's nightlife, the Jagdish Coffee Hotel.

This was not a hotel at all, but a one-room café open to the street. The kitchen received a constant supply of firewood, water, vegetables and milk,

and delivered an equally constant supply of great food. We grew especially fond of the two dishes on these pages, the spinach and potato dish saag aloo, and vegetable masala.

The Bay of Bengal at Gopalpur-on-Sea

MIXED VEGETABLE MASALA

This is a basic mixed-vegetable masala, using fried whole spices, chopped vegetables and tomatoes. The vegetables used can vary according to taste and availability.

SERVES 4–6

6 tablespoons sunflower oil

2 teaspoons black mustard seeds

2 teaspoons cumin seeds

2 teaspoons coriander seeds

6 fresh green chillies, chopped

12 garlic cloves, crushed

1 onion, thinly sliced

5 cm/2 inch piece of root ginger, peeled and finely chopped

1 teaspoon ground turmeric

2 medium carrots, cut into quarters lengthwise, then chopped

2 medium courgettes, cut into quarters lengthwise, then chopped

125 g/4 oz long green beans, cut into thirds

450 g/1 lb white cabbage, cut into 2.5 cm/1 inch squares

225 g/8 oz green peas (fresh or frozen)

225 g/8 oz tomatoes, chopped

handful of chopped coriander stalks, reserving leaves for garnish

2 tablespoons tomato purée

Get the oil very hot in a large heavy pan, then fry – in this order – the mustard seeds, cumin, coriander, chillies, garlic, onion, ginger and turmeric, adding each in rapid succession so the seeds have enough time to pop without burning.

When the onion begins to soften, add all the remaining vegetables except the tomatoes, together with the coriander stalks, and fry for a few minutes, until the cabbage begins to brown and the other vegetables soften.

Add the tomatoes and cook for 1 minute more. Add the tomato purée and reduce the heat, adding a little water to allow the vegetables to simmer until cooked.

Serve with rice and the coriander stalk leaves as a garnish.

SOUTHERN INDIA

Southern India includes the Deccan plateau, the plains of the Malabar and Coromandel coasts and the mountainous Eastern and Western Ghats that separate them, and, in the far south, the flat lands of Tamil Nadu. While the food of the coasts inevitably involves a lot of seafood, vegetarian options are still plentiful; in Tamil Nadu, as in Gujarat, vegetarianism is the norm. Much use is made of coconut in creamy sauces and nutty chutneys; rice grows everywhere and is served in copious amounts at every meal. The Deccan does not have the wealth that the coastal states have accumulated through generations of sea-trading, so the food there is often more basic. The exception is Bangalore, the capital of Karnataka, which has blossomed into a dynamic and prosperous city on the back of its booming information technology industry. Its new wealth has attracted India's first Kentucky Fried Chicken outlet and many fast-food imitators, but thankfully there has been demand for fine new Indian restaurants too.

We left Bangalore by the night train for the north of Karnataka, where, after a first-rate thali and a good night's sleep, we woke up to find an India from another century. We drove past acres of sunflowers to the sleepy town of Badami, whose tree-lined avenues were almost devoid of motorized traffic; bullock-carts, horse-drawn tongas and bicycles were the only company for our car. In the cliffs above the town are some fifth-century caves full of exquisite stone-carving depicting scenes from Hindu and Buddhist mythology. As the Moguls fought their way south in the sixteenth century destroying such images, they missed these, which are almost intact today. Despite such treasures, relatively few foreigners pass through Badami and tourists are still a novelty. From Badami we drove south to the ruins of Vijayanagar at Hampi: these have not survived years of conflict as well as Badami has, but their sheer size and their setting among desolate, boulder-strewn hills make them just as impressive.

In Kerala vegetables come immersed in fragrant coconut cream laced with spices, while in Tamil Nadu we ate well on numerous fill-up thalis, served on a fresh banana leaf. As soon as any one of the many ingredients on the leaf is eaten a man appears and replaces it with more of the same: only when one folds over the leaf is there an escape from the unending meal. However, more than the plethora of vegetable and dal dishes, it is the chutneys and raitas that we remember most, and we have given the tastiest of them in this chapter.

An elephant in the morning mists in Tamil Nadu's Mudumalai Sanctuary

POTATO AND PEANUT PAWA

Pawa is a type of flat rice available from Indian shops.

SERVES 4–6

4 tablespoons oil	1 green chilli, finely chopped
1 teaspoon black mustard seeds	1 tablespoon desiccated coconut
60 g/2 oz peanuts	salt
3 medium potatoes, cut into small	sugar
cubes and boiled until soft	125 g/4 oz pawa (dried flat rice),
1 teaspoon sesame seeds	rinsed and drained
½ teaspoon ground turmeric	large handful of fresh coriander
½ teaspoon chilli powder	leaves

Heat the oil in a large frying pan, add the mustard seeds and cook until they pop, then add the peanuts. When they begin to brown, add the drained potatoes, sesame seeds and turmeric. Fry until the potatoes begin to brown. Add the chilli powder, green chilli and coconut, with salt and sugar to taste; mix gently.

Remove from heat and mix in the pawa flakes. Return to the heat and fry until the pawa flakes are heated through.

Add the coriander leaves and either eat warm or keep in a sealed container for your train journey.

CACHUMBERS

A cachumber is a raw vegetable accompaniment that usually includes onion: we give the classic version with tomato.

SERVES 4–6

1 medium-to-large red onion, finely	1 tablespoon coriander leaves,
diced	chopped
3 tomatoes, cut into small cubes	salt
juice of 1 lime	

Mix all the ingredients in a bowl with salt to taste.

In the town of Badami we found people friendly and hospitable — so much so that when we enthused about a lunch we ate in a café, we were not allowed to pay for it. The day we left Badami we persuaded the café owners to let us pay for a tiffin tin full to take away with us. The dish was very simple, using an ingredient we had seen often in markets but never known how to use. This was pawa — dried flattened flakes of rice.

Quite unappetizing in its raw state, once brought to life with oil, spices, potatoes and peanuts, pawa becomes a great snack food. It is very popular in southern India — families cook it up and take it with them in stainless steel tins to snack on during long train journeys.

The entrance to the cave temples at Badami in Karnataka

COCONUT CABBAGE

SERVES 4–6

4 tablespoons sunflower oil

5 cm/2 inch piece of root ginger, peeled and cut into thin matchstick strips

2 green chillies, thinly sliced

8 curry leaves

1 level dessertspoon black mustard seeds

½ teaspoon ground turmeric

1 small white cabbage, finely shredded (about 675 g/1½ lb)

2 tablespoons desiccated coconut

1 teaspoon sugar

1 teaspoon salt

Make sure you have all the ingredients ready to throw in. Heat the sunflower oil in a wok and, when hot, add the ginger, chilli and curry leaves. Fry for a minute.

Add the mustard seeds and turmeric, and when the mustard seeds start to 'pop' add the cabbage. Stirring constantly, fry until the cabbage starts to wilt.

Add the coconut, stirring well until it begins to toast. Finally add the sugar and salt. Serve immediately.

The chickpea dish given here may be described as chana batura or chana masala. As chana batura, it is served with deep-fried batura bread and makes a popular fast-food dish in Bombay cafés. As chana masala, it can be a side-dish, along with vegetables and rice or chapatis, and appears all over India.

CHANA IN A THICK SPICY GRAVY

SERVES 4–6

handful of coriander leaves, chopped
handful of fresh mint, chopped
3 medium onions
12 garlic cloves
5 cm/2 inch piece of root ginger
1 teaspoon whole cumin seeds
1 teaspoon whole coriander seeds
5 cm/2 inch piece of cinnamon stick
7 dried red chillies
10 black peppercorns
2 bay leaves
1 teaspoon ground turmeric
4 tablespoons ghee
2 tablespoons tomato purée
250 g/9 oz dried chickpeas, soaked overnight and boiled until soft
2 medium potatoes, boiled and chopped small
300 g/10 oz spinach, chopped
salt

In a food processor, process the coriander, mint, onions, garlic and ginger to a paste.

Dry-roast the cumin and coriander seeds, cinnamon, chillies. peppercorns, bay leaves and turmeric in a dry frying pan over a medium heat, tossing continuously to avoid burning, then grind them all in a spice grinder into a dry masala.

Melt the ghee in a large heavy pan and fry the paste for 3 minutes. Add the dry masala and fry for another minute. Add the tomato purée and cook for 3 minutes more.

Add the drained chickpeas and chopped potatoes, followed by the spinach, and cook until the latter is wilted. Add water as needed to form a thick gravy. Season with salt to taste and serve.

A woman worships at the giant effigy of Ganesh, the elephant-headed Hindu god, at Hampi in northern Karnataka.

81

COCHIN COCONUT MASALA

SERVES 4–6

5 dried red chillies	1 teaspoon ground turmeric
2 tablespoons white poppy seeds	12 curry leaves
2 tablespoons coriander seeds	1 large onion, thinly sliced
1 teaspoon cumin seeds	1 large sweet potato, cut into
5 cloves	chunky 'chip' shapes
10 black peppercorns	2 medium courgettes, cut into
60 g/2 oz desiccated coconut,	'chips'
dry-roasted in a hot pan until	250 g/9 oz mooli, cut into 'chips'
just brown	125 g/4 oz okra, cut in half
6 tablespoons sunflower oil	lengthwise
1 teaspoon black mustard seeds	125 g/4 oz green beans, cut in half
1 teaspoon cumin seeds	400 ml/14 fl oz canned coconut
pinch of hing (asafoetida)	milk
5–10 green chillies, cut into thin	juice of 1 lime
strips	salt

Dry-roast the red chillies, poppy seeds, coriander seeds, cumin seeds, cloves and peppercorns, then grind them all in a spice grinder. Mix with the roasted coconut and a little water to make a paste.

Heat the oil in a large heavy pan. When hot, fry the mustard seeds, cumin seeds, hing, green chillies, turmeric and curry leaves, then add the onion. Fry until the onion is soft. Add the sweet potato and fry for 3 minutes.

Add the spice paste and all the other vegetables, stirring everything for 5 minutes. Then add the coconut milk, reduce the heat and cook until the vegetables are tender, adding a little water if necessary to keep things loose.

Finally, add the lime juice and a little salt to taste.

After a minor accident in Cochin in Kerala, I spent a night in hospital. The next day my bed was needed for another patient so I had to transfer to a hotel, but I was told not to walk for three days. I was borne aloft on a stretcher through the streets until a suitable hotel was found.

I hadn't considered the complication of getting food without being able to walk — but I needn't have worried. Each day medical students arrived to change my dressing and supply me with fresh food from their canteen, assuring me that it was merely their duty to attend the wounded.

While I was laid up in bed, this dish was something I looked forward to every day. I loved the way the vegetables were cut, as well as the tastes — it felt as if someone was really looking after me.

Enormous Chinese-style fishing nets, used in Cochin, are seen here silhouetted against the evening sky.

FRUIT LASSI

This refreshing and cooling yoghurt drink makes a perfect accompaniment to a spicy curry, and can be sweet or savoury. In the café we use mango, but you can use any soft fruit, such as banana.

SERVES 4–6

500 g / 1 lb 2 oz full-fat yoghurt
300 ml / ½ pint iced water
300 ml / ½ pint cold milk
½ teaspoon ground cardamom seeds

1 tablespoon rosewater
2 mangoes, peeled and cubed, or
5 ripe bananas, peeled and sliced
flaked roasted almonds, to serve

Place all the ingredients in a blender or food processor and blend until smooth. Serve with ice cubes and sprinkled with the flaked roasted almonds.

GREEN COCONUT CHUTNEY

SERVES 4–6

handful of coriander leaves

handful of mint leaves

1 garlic clove

2.5 cm/1 inch piece of root ginger, peeled and roughly chopped

2 green chillies

250 g/9 oz desiccated coconut

juice of 2 limes

1 teaspoon sugar

1 teaspoon salt

In a food processor, blend the coriander, mint, garlic, ginger, chilli, coconut and lime juice until they form a paste. Add just enough water to make a moist (but not wet) chutney. Mix in the sugar and salt.

If you are making this in advance, the coconut will absorb the water, so simply add more water to get the desired consistency before serving.

SWEET DATE AND TAMARIND CHUTNEY

SERVES 4–6

250 g/9 oz dates, chopped

1 level dessertspoon tamarind paste

1 dessertspoon cumin seeds, dry-roasted in a hot pan

1 teaspoon honey

salt

Place all the ingredients in a food processor with 250 ml/9 fl oz water and salt to taste, and blend until well combined.

In India no meal is complete without a chutney. There are hundreds of different recipes, for both fresh and cooked versions. Chutneys based on coconut are more common in the south, fruit chutneys in the north and west.

Raita is the term used for a variety of cooling yoghurt-based accompaniments. We've chosen two examples, one savoury, one sweet.

CUCUMBER AND MINT RAITA

SERVES 4–6

250 ml/9 fl oz yoghurt

½ cucumber, peeled and cut into small cubes

4 sprigs of mint, leaves removed and chopped

¼ teaspoon ground cumin

½ teaspoon sugar

salt and pepper

paprika

Whisk the yoghurt with a little water to thin it to a spoonable consistency. Add all of the remaining ingredients, except the paprika, with salt and pepper to taste. Mix well.

Chill the raita if you have the time. Sprinkle the paprika over the top before serving.

BANANA RAITA

SERVES 4–6

250 ml/9 fl oz yoghurt

1 teaspoon black mustard seeds

3 bananas, cut into 1 cm/½ inch rounds

½ teaspoon sugar

1 green chilli, thinly sliced

salt

Whisk the yoghurt with a little water to thin it to a spoonable consistency. Dry-roast the black mustard seeds until they start to pop (cover the pan to prevent them jumping out). Add to the yoghurt with all the remaining ingredients and salt to taste. Mix well.

WESTERN INDIA

The western states of Rajasthan and Gujarat are, perhaps, the most visually exciting in India. The stark beauty of desert landscapes is offset by brightly dressed women adorned with elaborate jewellery, and fine-featured men with noble moustaches and multi-coloured turbans. Fairy-tale palaces and dramatic forts dominate towns of tiny blue, pink and white houses squeezed together in narrow alleys. In the countryside, thatched mud huts have dung-floor courtyards populated with buffalo, camels and goats.

Desert culture is experienced in all its glory at the annual Camel Mela (fair) and Hindu pilgrimage in the oasis village of Pushkar. The ingredients are seductive: tens of thousands of Rajasthanis in all their finery, almost as many camels in theirs, a holy lake surrounded by temples, long days of sunshine, and nights of moonlit skies and festivities. The first time I went, my companion and I left our passports behind for safety in our Delhi hotel — breaching a law that requires foreigners to carry their documents. On being discovered without passports, we were arrested. Thus began a two-week ordeal.

For several days we were kept in an overcrowded cell, manacled hand and foot, and very worried. We were then taken in chains under police escort back to Delhi, an eighteen-hour train journey that we spent locked to the luggage rack. Even once our passports were found to be in order, we were told we had to return to the desert to be sentenced for the crime of not carrying them with us. Meanwhile, we had a day to spend in Delhi. None of our three police escorts had been to the capital before. A bargain was struck. We would give them a day out in the city and buy some presents for their wives, and they would put our chains in a bag. A good day was had by all.

Back in Pushkar we were given a clean cell all to ourselves — and were treated to fine feasts, delivered from the kitchens of our new friends' wives. At our trial we pleaded guilty and were released unconditionally. The policemen now insisted we stay on as guests in their homes. We met their wives, proudly dressed in the saris and bangles from Delhi, and complimented them on their cooking. With a mix of Hindi, English, and much pointing and laughing we gathered some of the recipes in this chapter.

Some of our trips produce pleasures less fraught with excitement. One of the most interesting parts of Rajasthan we visited is Shekhawati — a sand-blown region, home in the fourteenth century to prosperous Muslim merchants who built great mansions, or *havelis*, lavishly decorated with carvings and murals. Later generations abandoned these desert homes for the more sophisticated pleasures of the cities. Today the *havelis* are occupied by caretakers or local families, and most, sadly, are in a serious state of neglect.

The Pushkar Camel Mela (fair)

The Rann of Kutch is a wild district of Gujarat bordering Pakistan. The desert tribes are semi-nomadic, travelling in family groups with camels and goats. The capital, Bhuj, feels like a town from another century, although it is only three hours by air from Bombay. On our way back to Bombay, we stopped in Junagadh to climb the 10,000 stone steps up the temple-strewn Girnar Hill. Our ascent coincided with the festival of Shivaratri and its tens of thousands of pilgrims — many of them naked, ash-covered *sadhus* (holy men) who were not at all keen on being photographed. It was hard even to see a patch of ground in the throng of humanity, and the climb seemed quite effortless as the great crowd swept us with it up the mountain.

SAAG PANEER

This spinach and cheese dish is our all-time favourite recipe and we have eaten it in practically every state in India. There are many ways of cooking it, but in our opinion this is the best. The Indian cheese paneer is pretty tasteless in its raw state, but fried and soaked in sauce it is fantastic. Paneer is widely available in good supermarkets or in Indian stores.

SERVES 4–6

- 1 kg/2¼ lb fresh spinach, shredded
- 3–4 tablespoons ghee or butter (or sunflower oil)
- 400 g/14 oz paneer, cut into 1 cm/½ inch cubes
- 6 garlic cloves, crushed
- 5 cm/2 inch cube of root ginger, peeled and crushed
- 4 green chillies, finely chopped
- 1 dessertspoon garam masala
- ¼ teaspoon freshly grated nutmeg
- 250 ml/9 fl oz double cream
- large handful of coriander leaves, chopped
- salt

Cook the spinach with a small quantity of water, just enough to stop it from sticking, until wilted. Remove from heat.

Melt the ghee or butter, or heat the oil, in a heavy-based saucepan and fry the paneer until it is golden brown, turning it occasionally to make sure all sides are cooked.

With a slotted spoon, remove the paneer from the pan. Add the garlic, ginger and chillies to the saucepan (there should be enough ghee, butter or oil left in the pan, if not simply add a little more). Fry for 1 minute, stirring constantly.

Add the cooked spinach and any liquid that has come out of the spinach. Stir and simmer for 10 minutes.

Add the fried paneer back to the pan, together with the garam masala and nutmeg. Simmer for a further 10 minutes.

Finally add the double cream, chopped coriander leaves and salt to taste. Gently simmer for 5 minutes.

Serve with Raita (page 85) and rice cooked with cinnamon, cardamom and cloves (2.5 cm/1 inch piece of cinnamon stick, 3 cardamom pods and 3 cloves for 500 g/1 lb 2 oz of rice).

At the luxurious end of the comfort scale, we photographed royal palaces in Rajasthan and Gujarat that have been converted into Heritage Hotels. Some of these are former residences of undiluted opulence, others more modest ancestral homes.

In the superbly romantic courtyard of Shiv Niwas Palace in Udaipur we ate one of the best saag paneer dishes we tasted in India — substantially better than the meal we had the following night in the more famous and absurdly picturesque Lake Palace Hotel.

Saag Paneer

AN ALOO GOBI OF RAJASTHAN

SERVES 4–6

4 tablespoons ghee or butter (or
    sunflower oil)
pinch of hing (asafoetida)
pinch of fenugreek seeds
1 teaspoon fennel seeds
handful of fresh fenugreek leaves,
    finely chopped
handful of fresh coriander stalks,
    finely chopped

6 fresh green chillies, finely chopped
1 teaspoon ground turmeric
1 medium head of cauliflower,
    separated into florets and
    parboiled
3 medium potatoes, cubed and
    parboiled
salt and pepper

Aloo gobi (cauliflower and potato) is one of the ubiquitous dishes of India; it comes in hundreds — probably thousands — of forms. In fact, as the name suggests, cauliflower and potato are the only essential ingredients; beyond these the possibilities are endless.

Heat the ghee in a heavy pan and put in the hing, fenugreek seeds and fennel seeds. After 1 minute, add the fresh fenugreek and coriander; the ghee will spit as these fry, so the pan will need to be covered with a lid for a few seconds.

Add the chillies and turmeric with the parboiled cauliflower and potato, and stir around to coat these in ghee. Add salt and pepper to taste and a little water to loosen the mixture enough to simmer on a low heat, covered with a lid, until all is cooked.

Above **Brightly dressed women in a Rajasthani marketplace**
Right **The blue houses of Jodhpur seen through a narrow window in the Red Fort**

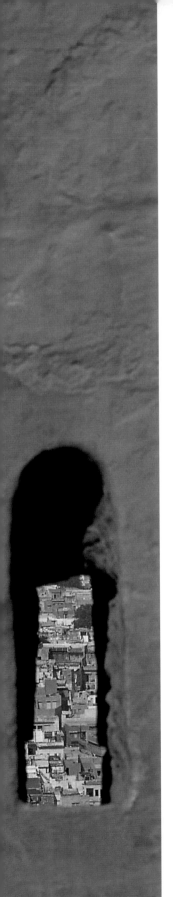

ROOT VEGETABLES IN A SPICY MINT SAUCE

We enjoyed this dish in Udaipur, on the banks of the lake overlooking the Lake Palace. You can use any root vegetable, but plenty of fresh mint is essential. Serve with rice and the Savoury Fruit Salad on page 95.

SERVES 4–6

4 teaspoons coriander seeds

1 teaspoon ground turmeric

2 teaspoons cayenne pepper

5 cm/2 inch cube of root ginger, peeled and roughly chopped

5 tablespoons sunflower oil

6 medium turnips, cubed

4 medium potatoes, cubed

6 medium tomatoes, puréed in a food processor

2 large handfuls of mint leaves, chopped

small handful of coriander leaves, chopped

salt

Dry-roast the coriander seeds in a hot small pan until they start to brown, then grind to a powder.

Place the ground coriander, turmeric, cayenne and ginger in a food processor and blend with a little water until a paste forms.

Heat the oil in a pan. When it is hot, fry the turnips and potatoes until they start to soften. Add the spice paste and stir until the vegetables are coated. Add the tomatoes and a little water to make a sauce. Simmer until the vegetables are nice and soft.

Add the mint and coriander with salt to taste. Stir to combine and serve immediately.

DEEP-RED RAJASTHANI VEGETABLES IN A POPPY-SEED SAUCE

In this unusual dish red cabbage, pumpkin, beetroot and a spice mixture based on chillies and paprika combine to make a dish of vivid colour, like the colours of Rajasthan itself. Poppy seeds are used to thicken the sauce.

SERVES 4–6

1 teaspoon fenugreek seeds

3 dessertspoons white poppy seeds

1 tablespoon sweet paprika

1 teaspoon ground coriander

1 teaspoon amchoor

1 teaspoon ground turmeric

1 teaspoon ground cinnamon

½ teaspoon ground cloves

5 cm/2 inch piece of root ginger, peeled and finely chopped

5 tablespoons sunflower oil

1 red onion, thinly sliced

4 garlic cloves, crushed

4–5 red chillies, thinly sliced

400 g/14 oz trimmed pumpkin, cut into cubes

5 medium raw beetroot, peeled and cubed

⅓ small red cabbage, thinly shredded

6 medium tomatoes, puréed in a food processor

2.5 cm/1 inch square of jaggery or 1 dessertspoon brown sugar

salt

chopped coriander leaves, to garnish

In a hot pan, dry-roast the fenugreek seeds until they start to brown. Remove from the heat and add to the poppy seeds. Grind these in a spice grinder or using a pestle and mortar. Combine with all the remaining spices and ginger.

Heat the oil in a large pan and, when hot, add the red onion, garlic and chilli. Fry these for a few minutes. Add the pumpkin, beetroot and red cabbage, and fry until they start to soften. Add the spice mix and stir until the vegetables are coated. Add the puréed tomatoes and a little water until the sauce just covers the vegetables. Bring to the boil and simmer until the vegetables are soft and the sauce has reduced. Add the jaggery or brown sugar and salt to taste. Stir to dissolve the sugar.

Garnish with chopped coriander and serve with rice and Banana Raita (page 85).

Deep-red Rajasthani Vegetables in a Poppy-seed Sauce

KHADI

We love khadi, which is a kind of yoghurt soup, but we always imagined it would be difficult to make as the tastes seem to be so complex and intriguing. In fact it's very easy, the secret being the blending of yoghurt with gram flour (*besan*). Khadi makes a good starter or addition to any rice and vegetable meal.

SERVES 4–6

500 ml/18 fl oz thick yoghurt
1½ tablespoons gram flour
4 green chillies, chopped
2.5 cm/1 inch piece of root ginger, finely chopped
2 teaspoons salt
2 teaspoons sugar
2 tablespoons ghee or butter (or sunflower oil)

½ teaspoon black mustard seeds
½ teaspoon fenugreek seeds
½ teaspoon cumin seeds
½ teaspoon ground turmeric
6 cloves
1 tablespoon curry leaves
pinch of hing (asafoetida)
handful of coriander leaves, chopped

In a large bowl, whisk together the yoghurt, gram flour, green chillies, ginger, salt and sugar with 1.5 litres/2¾ pints of water. Pour into a heavy pan, bring to the boil and simmer for 20 minutes on a low heat.

In a small pan, melt the ghee and fry all the seeds until they pop. Add the turmeric, cloves, curry leaves and hing. After 30 seconds, add all this to the yoghurt mixture, together with the coriander leaves. Stir and serve.

SAVOURY FRUIT SALAD

This is a zingy salad that makes a perfect accompaniment to a sweet, spicy curry.

SERVES 4–6

2 apples, cored and diced
2 carrots, cubed
2 oranges, peeled and cut into small cubes
½ cucumber, cubed
1 papaya, peeled, deseeded and cut into small cubes
juice of 1 lemon

handful of coriander leaves, chopped
1 teaspoon cumin seeds, dry-roasted and ground
½ teaspoon amchoor
½ teaspoon freshly ground black pepper
salt

A camel trader in Pushkar

Simply combine all ingredients and chill for about 30 minutes before serving to allow flavours to combine.

GUJARATI CARROT SALAD

SERVES 4–6

1 level dessertspoon black mustard
   seeds
4 carrots, grated
1 teaspoon salt

juice of 2 limes
handful of mint leaves, roughly
   chopped

First dry-roast the mustard seeds in a hot pan until they start to 'pop' (cover the
pan with a lid or plate to prevent them jumping out). Remove from the heat
and, when cool, combine with all the remaining ingredients.

GUJARATI PUMPKIN WITH TAMARIND

This Gujarati dish blends the sweetness of pumpkin and jaggery with the sourness of tamarind and amchoor. It works well served with Coconut Cabbage (page 79) and Date and Tamarind Chutney (page 84).

SERVES 4–6 WITH ACCOMPANIMENTS

4 garlic cloves

3 red chillies

1 red onion, roughly chopped

1 heaped teaspoon coriander seeds

1 dessertspoon tamarind paste

1 dessertspoon jaggery or brown sugar

3 tablespoons of boiling water

3 tablespoons ghee or butter (or sunflower oil)

1 large onion, thinly sliced

1 kg/2¼ lb pumpkin, peeled, deseeded and cubed

½ teaspoon ground turmeric

½ teaspoon ground black pepper

1 level teaspoon amchoor

salt

large handful of coriander leaves, chopped

Place the garlic, chillies and red onion in a blender or food processor and blend to a paste.

In a small pan, dry-roast the coriander seeds until they start to turn golden-brown, then grind to a powder.

Dissolve the tamarind paste and jaggery or brown sugar in the boiling water.

In a large pan, melt the ghee or butter or heat the oil. Add the onion and fry until it starts to soften. Add the pumpkin and fry until it starts to brown, stirring occasionally.

Add the garlic, onion and chilli paste, the ground coriander, turmeric and black pepper. Stir well and fry for a few seconds. Add the tamarind and jaggery water and 250 ml/9 fl oz more water. Simmer gently, with the lid on, until the pumpkin is soft and most of the water has evaporated (but if it gets too dry at any time, add a little more water).

Add the amchoor, salt to taste and chopped coriander leaves, stir and simmer for 3 more minutes. Serve.

DIU SWEETCORN CURRY

Coconut milk is a perfect accompaniment to corn cobs. This curry is delicious served with Gujarati Carrot Salad (page 96) and fresh mango chutney, or, for a larger meal, with the Gujarati Pumpkin (page 97) as well.

SERVES 4–6

6 corn cobs, cut into 2.5 cm/1 inch rounds

2 large handfuls of coriander leaves, chopped, plus more to garnish

4 green chillies

5 cm/2 inch piece of root ginger, peeled and chopped

2 garlic cloves

2 heaped tablespoons desiccated coconut

200 ml/7 fl oz coconut milk

2 tablespoons ghee or butter (or sunflower oil)

1 dessertspoon black mustard seeds

10 curry leaves

salt

Cook the corn cobs in boiling salted water until they start to soften. Drain and place back in the pan.

In a food processor, blend the coriander leaves, chillies, ginger, garlic and desiccated coconut to a paste. Add the paste to the corn cobs with enough water to make a sauce. Bring to the boil, reduce the heat and simmer, covered, for 10 minutes. Add the coconut milk and gently simmer for 5 minutes more.

Meanwhile, melt the ghee in a small pan and add the mustard seeds. When they start to 'pop' (a matter of seconds), add the curry leaves. Remove from heat and pour over the curry – it will make quite a loud crackling noise, so stand back a little. Add salt to taste and garnish with more coriander leaves.

Diu, a small island in the Arabian Sea, is just offshore from India's last 'dry' state, Gujarat, but has a decidedly European taste for the pleasures of beer, wine and spirits bequeathed to it by its long Portuguese history. Diu's pastel houses, narrow cobbled lanes, tavernas and beaches are more reminiscent of the Mediterranean than India.

We discovered this dish while trying to drag ourselves away from the island after a welcome rest. A long-delayed train resulted in the station-master's inviting us to lunch in his home, and we ate with the family in a cobalt-blue courtyard just behind the station. We were quite disappointed when our train eventually arrived.

Diu Sweetcorn Curry, with Gujarati Carrot Salad (page 96)

NEPAL

The tourist 'ghetto' of Thamil in Kathmandu offers a cosmopolitan choice of cuisine. Cafés, bistros and restaurants line the streets to compete for the lucrative trade of hungry trekkers. On the most popular routes tiny Himalayan villages provide banana pancakes, 'Swiss' rostis and pumpkin pie. In the remoter valleys the choice is reduced to the Nepalese mainstay of dal bhaat subji, basic dal, rice and vegetables. In the fertile lower valleys these meals can be magnificent concoctions of creamy dals, healthy vegetables, good clean rice and a range of chutneys and pickles. With increasing altitude and harshness of conditions the choice of vegetables diminishes, and rice is more coarse. Altitude finally prevents rice cultivation altogether, and vegetarian meals consist of little more than potatoes with chillies and *tsampa* porridge. Even in such places, where life appears a constant battle against the elements, trekking in Nepal is made a pleasure by the warmth and good humour of the people as much as by the stunning landscapes.

Marigolds bloom under the Annapurna peaks.

We ate dal bhaat in one form or another every day during a six-week circumnavigation of the Annapurna Mountains, and never got bored with it.

As rice was usually the cheapest ingredient in these meals, there was always plenty of it. To stretch the vegetable and dal dishes, they were made very spicy so that only a little was needed with each mouthful of rice.

In village homes, the meal is always eaten by mixing a little dal and vegetable or pickle with some rice and scooping it up with the right hand.

ANNAPURNA DAL BHAAT

This recipe is simple and a good way of making a lot of food relatively quickly.

SERVES 4–6

For the dal

4 tablespoons ghee or butter (or sunflower oil)

2 medium onions, thinly sliced

5 cm/2 inch piece of root ginger, finely chopped

9 garlic cloves, crushed

2 teaspoons dried red chillies, crushed

1 teaspoon ground turmeric

300 g/10 oz red lentils

salt

For the vegetables (subji)

6 tablespoons sunflower oil

9 fresh green chillies, cut into thin strips

5 cm/2 inch piece of root ginger, finely chopped

1 teaspoon ground cumin

1 teaspoon ground coriander seeds

½ teaspoon chilli powder

1 teaspoon ground turmeric

6 small new potatoes, cut into 1 cm/½ inch slices

3 medium carrots, cut into quarters lengthwise and chopped

1 small cauliflower, cut into small florets

250 g/9 oz shelled peas

First prepare the dal: melt the ghee in a large heavy pan and, when hot, fry the onions, ginger and garlic until soft. Then add the chillies and turmeric, and fry for a minute more. Add the lentils and stir to coat them in the spices, then add enough water to cover them. Bring to the boil, lower the heat and simmer until the lentils are cooked, about 30 minutes, adding more water if necessary at any time to keep the dal the consistency of a thickish soup. Season with salt to taste.

Towards the end of the lentil cooking time, cook the vegetables: heat the oil in a large heavy pan. When hot, fry the chillies, ginger and spices for 1 minute, stirring continuously. Add all the vegetables except the peas and cook until they begin to soften. Then add the peas with a little water and cook over a lower heat until they are tender.

Serve with plenty of steamed rice, any favourite pickles and a salad of sliced daikon, fresh coriander leaves and chopped red onion.

SRI LANKA

Sri Lanka is a remarkably beautiful and deeply troubled island. Yet, considering the scale of the violence that is a daily reality for so many Sri Lankans, it is incredibly easy to be temporarily unaware of any trouble. We spent two weeks driving around the island's enchanting landscapes, meeting gentle, polite people, visiting serene Buddhist temple sites hosted by saffron-robed monks, or lazing on palm-fringed beaches. Nonetheless, there were sinister reminders of the island's tragedy lurking in the background, and our time was punctuated with police roadblocks, restricted travel and an atmosphere of tension.

Self-drive car hire is difficult in Sri Lanka, so we shared our trip with a driver. There is a certain relief in being freed from the stress of driving in a foreign country, but it can be a complicated equation having to share almost every hour of every day with a man you have never met before. Our driver, Cyril, took his job very seriously: he was a faultless chauffeur, always smartly turned out and punctual. In fact, he took everything very seriously, and seemed to be bored beyond words by yet another drive around the island with a couple of excitable tourists — that is, until we declared our intention of climbing to the summit of Adam's Peak. The ascent of Adam's Peak is a demanding pilgrimage of which, as a devout Buddhist, Cyril thoroughly approved. At the 2,223 metre (7,340 ft) summit of the pyramid-shaped mountain there is a large 'footprint' in the rock, left by the Buddha, or Adam, or St Thomas, or Shiva, or geology, depending on your preference.

We certainly earned Cyril's friendship. The climb lasted all night. When we set off in the relative cool of the evening, the almost party atmosphere among the ascending pilgrims and the lure of thousands of steps winding up the mountain lined by fairy-lights made a seductive combination. Several hours later in the chill of the pre-dawn air the romance was fading fast. Our energy was replenished by the spectacular sunrise — not to mention the excitement of seeing, just outside the summit temple, a bright red British Royal Mail-style pillarbox, with a daily collection at noon (which must demand an extremely fit postman). But then, disorientated as we were from lack of sleep, the descent, under an unrelenting tropical sun, down near-vertical steps, was punishing. We were as happy to see Cyril and his car waiting for us at the bottom as he had been to discover that his passengers were some sort of pilgrims.

A stilt fisherman at dusk in southern Sri Lanka

GREEN VEGETABLE MALLUNG

Mallung, which means 'mixed up', is also the name of curries made with curry leaves, coconut and chilli. Mallung is most commonly made with green vegetables, of which there are many in Sri Lanka. Broccoli, for example, is abundant. This recipe can be made with any green vegetables, so feel free to substitute.

Traditionally mallung should contain fish paste, made from pounded dried fish. In the café we do not, of course, use any fish products, but if you do eat fish, you might like to include Worcestershire sauce, which contains anchovies. The flavour is quite similar to that of fish paste, but more subtle.

SERVES 4–6

4 tablespoons sunflower oil	175 g/6 oz spinach, coarsely shredded
1 large red onion, thinly sliced	
4 green chillies, thinly sliced	400 ml/14 fl oz coconut milk
12 curry leaves	1 tablespoon Worcestershire sauce (optional)
1 tablespoon black mustard seeds	
350 g/12 oz broccoli florets	½ teaspoon ground saffron
350 g/12 oz peeled and cubed marrow	salt
	juice of 1 lime
60 g/2 oz desiccated coconut	chopped coriander leaves, to garnish

Heat the oil in a large pan and, when hot, add the onion and fry it for a few minutes, then add the chillies, curry leaves and mustard seeds. Fry until the mustard seeds 'pop'.

Add the broccoli, marrow and desiccated coconut, and stir until the vegetables are coated in the spices and the coconut is toasted. Pour over enough water partially to cover the vegetables and simmer until they are just starting to soften.

Stir in the spinach, the coconut milk, the Worcestershire sauce if you are using it, and the saffron. Gently simmer until all the vegetables are soft. Add salt to taste and the lime juice.

Garnish with coriander leaves and serve with Onion Sambol (page 111) and rice.

After we had earned the approval of our driver, Cyril, by our ascent of Adam's Peak, he made it his mission to search out the best food he could find, and eagerly explained how things were cooked. Lunch that day was a mallung, or mixture, of green vegetables in a coconut-cream sauce with black mustard seeds, green chillies, yellow saffron and fresh curry leaves.

We ate the mallung while enjoying a grand view down towards the coastal plains. It tasted so delicious that we wondered if the setting, together with the healthy appetite from all our exercise, might be deceiving our senses, but every time we have cooked this dish since, its excellence has been confirmed.

Green Vegetable Mallung

BEETROOT AND BRINJAL BLACK CURRY

This recipe works well with Toasted Coconut and Pineapple Chutney (page 108) and the combination of yellow and red looks wonderful.

SERVES 4–6

2 red onions, roughly chopped	450 g/1 lb raw beetroot (trimmed weight), peeled and cubed
3 garlic cloves	
3–4 hot red chillies (either dried and soaked or fresh)	5 baby aubergines (brinjal), cut into quarters
1 lemon grass stalk	200 ml/7 fl oz stock
1 dessertspoon cumin seeds	300 ml/½ pint coconut milk
1 dessertspoon coriander seeds	salt and pepper
1 scant teaspoon fennel seeds	125 g/4 oz cashew nuts
4 tablespoons sunflower oil	

In a food processor, process the onions, garlic, chillies and lemon grass to a pulp. Dry-roast the cumin, coriander and fennel seeds in a small pan until they are dark brown (but not burnt or they will taste bitter). Grind to a powder using a spice grinder or pestle and mortar.

Heat the oil in a large heavy pan. When hot, add the onion paste and cook briskly for a few minutes, then throw in the ground spices, stirring continuously. When the spices are combined with the onion paste, add the beetroot and aubergine. Fry for a further minute or two on high heat, stirring constantly.

Pour in the stock and bring to the boil, then reduce the heat, cover and simmer until the vegetables are nice and soft. Add the coconut milk and cook for a further 5 minutes. Meanwhile, dry-roast the cashew nuts until golden.

Season the curry to taste with salt and pepper. Garnish the curry with the toasted cashew nuts and serve with Toasted Coconut and Pineapple Chutney and Coconut Rice (page 108).

In Sri Lanka the main dishes are usually white curries, which are mild and creamy with lots of coconut milk; red curries, which are scarlet from ground chillies and tomatoes; or, delicious and most unusual-looking, black curries, darkened by spices roasted whole and ground to a powder.

We found this splendid recipe for Beetroot and Brinjal Black Curry at the delightfully 'olde worlde' New Oriental Hotel in Galle, on the west coast of Sri Lanka. Built in 1865 as an officers' barracks, the hotel is famous not only for its atmospheric Victorian interiors, but also for its food.

Hill country near Adam's Peak

COCONUT RICE

SERVES 4–6

500 g/1 lb 2 oz basmati rice
30 g/1 oz butter
1 red onion, thinly sliced
4 green cardamom pods, lightly
    crushed

300 ml/½ pint coconut milk
salt

Rinse the rice until the water runs clear.

Melt the butter in the pan in which you are going to cook the rice and fry the onion in it until softened. Add the cardamom and rice and stir until the rice is coated in the butter. Add the coconut milk and enough water to cover the rice by 1 cm/½ inch, with salt to taste.

Cover with a tight-fitting lid and bring to the boil, then reduce the heat and simmer gently until all water is absorbed.

Adjust the season if necessary, fluffing the rice with fork as you do so. Leave to stand for a further 10 minutes, still covered, before serving.

TOASTED COCONUT AND PINEAPPLE CHUTNEY

Pineapple works particularly well with chilli, producing a delicious combination of sweet and sour.

SERVES 4–6

60 g/2 oz desiccated coconut
½ medium pineapple, peeled, cored
    and cubed

3 hot green chillies, thinly sliced
juice of 1 lime
salt to taste

Dry-roast the desiccated coconut in a hot pan, stirring constantly, until it just starts to brown. Turn it out of the pan and set aside.

Combine the pineapple, chillies, lime juice and salt to taste. Pour this over the coconut, mix well and serve immediately.

Kandy is the capital of the hill country and, in many ways, it is also the spiritual capital. The Temple of the Tooth houses Sri Lanka's most important Buddhist relic, the Sacred Tooth of the Buddha, which is believed to have been taken from the flames of his funeral pyre and smuggled into Ceylon in the fourth century, hidden in the hair of a princess.

During morning and evening ceremonies it is possible to 'view' the tooth. In fact you only see one of the many layers of casket in which it is housed and, needless to say, it is very heavily guarded. We ate this delicious leek and potato curry after the 'viewing'.

KANDY LEEK AND POTATO CURRY

SERVES 4–6

1 heaped dessertspoon cumin seeds

1 heaped dessertspoon coriander seeds

1 teaspoon fennel seeds

4 tablespoons sunflower oil

1 red onion, thinly sliced

5 garlic cloves, crushed

5 cm/2 inch piece of root ginger, finely chopped

4 medium white potatoes, cubed and parboiled

4 large leeks, cut into 2.5 cm/1 inch slices

5 cm/2 inch piece of cinnamon stick

½ teaspoon turmeric

1 teaspoon chilli powder

8 curry leaves

1 tablespoon vinegar

300 ml/½ pint coconut milk

salt

fresh coriander leaves, to garnish

Dry-roast the cumin, coriander and fennel seeds in a small pan until they start to brown, then grind them to a powder using a spice grinder or pestle and mortar.

Heat the oil in a large heavy pan and, when hot, add the onion, garlic and ginger, and fry until soft. Add the potatoes and leeks and fry until the vegetables start to brown. Add the ground spice mix, cinnamon, turmeric, chilli powder, curry leaves and vinegar, stirring constantly to prevent sticking and ensuring that all the vegetables are coated in the spices.

Now add enough water barely to cover the vegetables and simmer gently until the vegetables soften. Add the coconut milk and simmer for a further 5 minutes.

Add salt to taste and sprinkle with the chopped coriander leaves. Serve with Coconut Sambol (page 111) and rice.

A young monk takes a photograph with my camera at the Buddhist cliff carvings at Polonnaruwa.

COCONUT SAMBOL

SERVES 4–6

85 g/3 oz desiccated coconut

6 shallots or 1 medium red onion, sliced

8 curry leaves

6 red chillies (fewer if you don't like it too spicy)

juice of 2 limes

salt

Soak the coconut in water until it swells and becomes fleshy. Place in a food processor with the remaining ingredients and salt to taste, then blend until well combined. If the mixture seems dry, simply add a little water.

You can store this sambal in an airtight container in the fridge for a few days. The coconut will continue to absorb any moisture, so re-moisten with a little lime juice and water before serving.

ONION SAMBOL

SERVES 4–6

3 tablespoons sunflower oil

3 medium onions, finely chopped

4 garlic cloves, crushed

2 green chillies, thinly sliced

2.5 cm/1 inch cube of root ginger, peeled and finely chopped

4 green cardamom pods, lightly crushed

1 teaspoon ground cinnamon

2 teaspoons garam masala

1 teaspoon salt

1 teaspoon brown sugar

1 tablespoon vinegar

150 ml/¼ pint tamarind water (2 tablespoons tamarind purée dissolved in 150 ml/¼ pint water)

1 tablespoon Worcestershire sauce (optional)

Heat the oil in a heavy pan. When hot, fry the onions, garlic, chillies and ginger until soft. Add all the spices and stir them into the onions.

Now add all remaining ingredients and gently simmer until the water content reduces to give a chutney-like consistency. In a food processor, purée the contents of the pan, but be sure to retain some 'bite'. This sambal can be stored in an airtight container in the fridge for up to a month.

Sambols are spicy dry chutneys. They are served as accompaniments to most meals or, as a light meal, simply with roti bread or hoppers (rice-flour pancakes).

Southeast Asia

& China

Southeast Asia & China

All the countries of this region have a strong tradition of creative cooking using vegetables, nuts, spices and soya bean products. The results are quite different from the dishes that dominate Indian cooking. Pulses are used much less, and soya beans appear in the guise of tofu, tempeh and of course soy sauce. Lemon grass, galangal and lime leaves are the dominant spices. When travelling through most of this region vegetarians can enjoy a great variety of dishes to accompany the ubiquitous staple of steamed white rice.

In some parts of the region travel is very easy. Our journeys around Bali and Lombok were made in the comfort of a private jeep, and we were never far from a luxury hotel. By contrast, in Burma, hours of travelling in overcrowded jeeps down forest tracks and mountain paths were rewarded by the sight of exquisite landscapes and encounters with some of the most welcoming people in Asia. Similarly in China, although it seemed that every day another complex negotiation was needed to enable us to continue our journey down the Li River, the beauty of the mountainous country compensated for any frustration. We were less fortunate in Laos, where all our attempts to travel beyond the capital were defeated by bureaucracy. But then in Borneo I was granted the ultimate privilege of travelling deep in virgin rainforest, where no human race has ever lived.

Not unexpectedly, of the countries in this chapter, it is Burma, bordering India, whose cuisine is most clearly influenced by the style of its larger neighbour, with its blending of Indian and Oriental styles. China can be the hardest of all these countries for a vegetarian to travel through. Its most interesting vegetarian dishes are from Buddhist cooking traditions, which are most easily accessible in the cosmopolitan environment of Hong Kong. Conversely, in Thailand, Malaysia and Indonesia it is rarely a problem to find sound vegetarian meals, although a tolerance of (or even a liking for) shrimp paste and fish sauce is a big bonus when it comes to enjoying street food. We have omitted such ingredients from the recipes in this chapter and used soy sauce instead. The complex flavours of all the other ingredients combine to make such exciting tastes that the fish flavours are hardly missed. The ingredients for Southeast Asian cooking are increasingly easy to find in supermarkets, although it's always worth stocking up on the basics when in a Chinese or Thai shop.

Pages 112-113 **The Huang Shan Mountains**
Right **Fresh vegetables piled high in a vegetable market in Burma**

BURMA

Life for the Burmese has changed since we last travelled there in the 1980s. At that time Burma offered one of the most fascinating travel experiences in Asia. The complications of seven-day visas, closed areas and unreliable transport were insignificant compared to the visual and cultural treats of a land so steeped in tradition and isolated from the outside. The flood plain of the Irrawaddy River at Pagan dotted with ancient pagodas; the leg-rowing fishermen of Ingle Lake; the giant reclining Buddha of Pegu; the golden spires of the Shwe Dagon pagoda; the morning mists over Rangoon harbour – all were the stuff of life-long memories.

And the food wasn't bad either. We ate dishes such as vegetables stir-fried with tamarind; cucumber and roasted sesame seed salads; and lemon grass rice. One day we would love to go back to Burma and see how much of the beauty we enjoyed so much has survived. Until then we have to make do with the memories and the food.

CUCUMBER AND SESAME SEED SALAD

SERVES 4–6

1 heaped tablespoon sesame seeds
1 tablespoon sunflower oil
2 red onions, thinly sliced
2 garlic cloves
1 large cucumber, peeled and cubed

For the dressing
2 tablespoons cider vinegar
½ teaspoon ground turmeric
1 generous teaspoon brown sugar
  or honey
2 tablespoons sesame oil
salt

Dry-roast the sesame seeds in a heavy pan until they start to 'pop', then set aside. Heat the sunflower oil in a frying pan and, when hot, fry the onions and garlic until caramelized and brown.

Make the dressing by slowly mixing the vinegar with the turmeric and sugar or honey, then stir in the sesame oil. Season to taste with salt.

Pour the dressing over the diced cucumber and top with the fried onions and garlic and toasted sesame seeds.

Shadowy boat traffic haunts Rangoon harbour at dawn.

116

LEMON GRASS RICE

Serves 4–6

1 small red onion, roughly chopped
2 garlic cloves
2 red chillies, roughly chopped
500 g/1 lb 2 oz basmati rice
salt
2 lemon grass stalks, cut down the middle and hit with a rolling pin
juice of 1 lime

Blend the onion, garlic and chillies in a food processor until a paste forms.

Rinse the rice until the water runs clear. Place it in a pan which has a tight-fitting lid and add enough water to cover by 1 cm/½ inch, with salt to taste. Add the lemon grass and bring to the boil. Cover, reduce the heat and simmer gently until all the water is absorbed.

Fluff the rice with a fork, at the same time stirring in the onion paste. Cook over a very low heat for a further 5 minutes. Squeeze over the lime juice and adjust the seasoning if necessary.

STIR-FRY IN TAMARIND GRAVY

Serves 4—6

1 red onion, roughly chopped

3 garlic cloves

3 fresh red chillies

2.5 cm/1 inch cube of root ginger, peeled and roughly chopped

2 lemon grass stalks, thinly sliced

2 teaspoons cumin seeds, dry-roasted and ground

1 teaspoon dark soy sauce or shrimp paste

2 tablespoons tamarind paste

3 tablespoons sunflower oil

bunch of spring onions, cut into 2 cm/¾ inch slices

2 carrots, cut into fine matchsticks

450 g/1 lb Chinese leaf, cut into 2.5 cm/1 inch strips

300 g/10 oz pak choy, coarsely cut

200 g/7 oz fine asparagus, cut into 7.5 cm/3 inch pieces

2 red peppers, deseeded and thinly sliced

1 dessertspoon brown sugar or honey

2 tablespoons shoyu or light soy sauce (optional)

salt

For the garnish

large handful of coriander leaves, chopped

large handful of beansprouts

In a food processor, blend the red onion, garlic, chilli, ginger, lemon grass, cumin and dark soy sauce or shrimp paste until a paste forms. Dissolve the tamarind paste in 300 ml/½ pint of hot water.

In a wok, heat the sunflower oil until hot. Add the onion paste and fry briskly for a few seconds, stirring to avoid sticking. Add the spring onions, carrots, Chinese leaf, pak choy, asparagus and red pepper. Stir-fry on a high heat until the vegetables are all coated in the paste and they start to soften. Gradually add the tamarind water, a little at a time, until the vegetables are just cooked.

Add the brown sugar or honey, shoyu or soy sauce if necessary and salt to taste. Garnish with coriander and beansprouts piled on top of the dish.

Pagan, on the flood plain of the Irrawaddy River, is like a setting for a fairy tale. Majestic temple ruins in their hundreds are scattered over the plains along the meandering river. When we were there only the most basic accommodation was available. After a long, hot, dusty day's cycling around the ruins we really enjoyed the Stir-Fry in Tamarind Gravy served by the family who ran our rustic guest-house.

After dinner the women of the house offered us a local-style massage, which involved their walking over our backs with animated vigour. They giggled so much as they did this that we half-suspected it to be a joke they played on passing foreigners.

Stir-fry in Tamarind Gravy

CHINA

Our one experience of China was a boat-journey down the Li Xian and Pearl rivers from Yangshuo to the South China Sea at Hong Kong — perhaps one of the most beautiful river journeys in the world. The Huang Shan Mountains around Yangshuo form the round-topped, sheer-sided shapes familiar from classical Chinese paintings. One night we slept in a cave near the summit of one of the hills so that we could photograph the dawn mists rising through the extraordinary landscape. During the day we hired bicycles to explore the rice paddies and villages between the peaks.

Southern China is a bit of a horror show for vegetarians. Most villages we stopped in had drab cafés where surly waiters threw frightening bowls of gruel down on dirty tables. Sometimes the 'menu' was a stack of cages stuffed with all kinds of animals, including rats, cats and owls. Some days we lived off boiled rice and raw peanuts.

We were relieved to get back to Hong Kong, one of the world's most interesting cities in which to discover unusual food. Some dishes use extraordinary ingredients such as tree moss and fermented gluten, while others are simple but enticing combinations of mushrooms or mixed vegetables in light sauces.

A rice paddy near Yangshuo

Several of Hong Kong's islands offer an almost rural escape from the intensity of the city. Lantau is not the quietest, but it is one of the most rewarding to visit. There is a good walk up to the hill-top monastery of Po Lin, where the monks invite visitors to eat lunch with them; it was at Po Lin that I first ate this dish of 'Buddhist meat' with shiitake mushrooms.

'BUDDHIST MEAT' AND SHIITAKE MUSHROOMS

'Buddhist meat' is a popular name for seitan or wheat gluten, which can be found in health-food stores and Chinese shops. If there is a problem getting hold of seitan, tofu can be used instead; the dry pre-cooked style works better than the more common wet style.

SERVES 4

5 tablespoons sunflower oil

2.5 cm/1 inch piece of root ginger, peeled and thinly sliced

3 garlic cloves, thinly sliced

250 g/9 oz shiitake mushrooms, quartered

4 medium carrots, cut into matchstick strips

bunch of spring onions, cut into 2.5 cm/1 inch pieces

salt and pepper

300 g/10 oz seitan or tofu, cut into strips

1 tablespoon hoisin sauce

1 tablespoon light soy sauce

1 tablespoon rice wine

1 teaspoon sesame oil

toasted sesame seeds, to serve

Heat 3 tablespoons of the sunflower oil in a wok and, when hot, fry half the ginger and half the garlic for about 20 seconds. Add the mushrooms, the carrots and most of the spring onions and toss in the hot oil for 2 minutes. Remove these vegetables, sprinkle with salt and set aside.

Wipe out the wok and heat the remaining oil. When hot, fry the seitan or tofu with the remaining garlic and ginger, until it begins to go brown on the outside.

Combine the hoisin sauce, soy sauce, rice wine, sesame oil and a little salt and pepper in a bowl with 4 tablespoons of water, then pour into the wok, returning the vegetables at the same time. Simmer gently for a few minutes.

Serve with steamed rice, the rest of the spring onions and toasted sesame seeds.

SOUTH CHINA STIR-FRY

This is a simple, healthy, clean-tasting combination of fresh vegetables cooked quickly in a little oil and flavoured with fresh ginger and rice wine. Any vegetables can be used.

SERVES 4–6

125 g/4 oz fresh asparagus

125 g/4 oz cauliflower florets

125 g/4 oz broccoli florets

4 tablespoons sunflower oil

7.5 cm/3 inch piece of root ginger, cut into fine matchstick strips

60 g/2 oz shiitake mushrooms

225 g/8 oz straw mushrooms (canned are fine)

125 g/4 oz sugar snap peas

125 g/4 oz baby sweetcorn, cut in half lengthwise

4 red chillies, cut into strips

2 teaspoons cornflour, mixed to a paste with a little water

2 tablespoons rice wine

2 tablespoons soy sauce

1 teaspoon salt

1 teaspoon sugar

finely chopped spring onions, to finish

Boil the asparagus, cauliflower and broccoli in salted water for 1 minute, then refresh in cold water and drain.

Heat the oil in a large wok until smoking, then add the ginger, all the vegetables and the chillies. Cook over a high heat, stirring continuously for 5 minutes.

Stir in all the remaining ingredients and serve with finely chopped spring onions sprinkled over, accompanied by rice.

In southern China we were 'slightly' arrested for being slightly off limits. It was a genuine mistake on our part, and a nervous provincial policeman decided that instead of putting us in the cells he would invite us to be guests in his home for the night, before sending us back to a town 'on limits'.

We managed to convey our desire for a meatless meal in time to save any embarrassment during the evening meal with his family. This stir-fry turned out to be the best meal we ate in China. The vegetables are simply those the policeman's wife found in the local market that day.

The distinctive peaks of the Huang Shan Mountains, towering over a tributary of the Li Xian River near Yangshuo

LAOS

In the late 1980s Laos began to open up after decades of isolation and, as we were in Thailand anyway, we decided to go and have a look. We specially wanted to visit the temple sites of the first Lao kingdom and the old French colonial mansions in Luang Phabang. The Laotian Embassy in Bangkok refused us visas, but we booked a two-week 'package', including visas, through a scruffy little tourist agency. We crossed the Mekong on a small ferry at dawn. The immigration officers seemed happy with our visas which, written in Lao script, meant nothing to us, and we struck up an acquaintance with a couple returning to Laos for the first time since escaping as refugees

Detail from a Buddhist temple in Vientiane

We first ate this stir-fry on the banks of the mighty Mekong River, at the village wedding feast we had been invited to by our new friends. The thickening of puréed aubergines is characteristic of Laotian dishes — aubergines are abundant in Laos.

fifteen years before. They were on their way to a village near Vientiane, the capital, for a family wedding, and with typical Asian hospitality they invited us to accompany them. We spent several enjoyable hours at the feast, sharing in the double celebration of the reunion and the wedding festivities, and eating vast quantities of delicious food.

That was the good bit. The next day, having reluctantly spent a night in our sombre pre-paid hotel in Vientiane, a compulsory part of the package, we tried to organize a flight or a boat-journey to Luang Phabang, only to find, to our dismay, that our visas were good only for Vientiane and, moreover, expired that day. There was no way of getting to Luang Phabang 'with visas like this'; we had no option but to return to the ferry. And that was all we saw of Laos.

MEKONG STIR-FRY WITH PUREED AUBERGINE

Serves 4—6

2 aubergines
3 tablespoons sunflower oil
6 spring onions, cut into
   2 cm / ¾ inch slices
3 garlic cloves, crushed
3 red chillies, thinly sliced
1 teaspoon fennel seeds, crushed
250 g / 9 oz shiitake mushrooms,
   thickly sliced

250 g / 9 oz fine green beans, cut in
   half
225 g / 8 oz spinach, shredded
225 g / 8 oz sugar snap peas
5 cm / 2 inch piece of galangal,
   peeled and thinly sliced
handful of fresh mint leaves
handful of fresh sweet basil leaves
salt

Make the aubergine purée: cut away the top of the aubergines and slice the rest in half lengthwise. Immerse these in boiling salted water and simmer until the flesh is soft. Remove from the pan and scoop the flesh from the skin using a spoon. Either mash the flesh using a potato masher or purée in a food processor. Set aside.

Heat the oil in a wok and, when hot, flash-fry the spring onions, garlic and chillies. Follow these with the fennel seeds, then add the shiitake and green beans, and stir-fry for a further minute or two. Add the shredded spinach and sugar snap peas, stirring constantly. Add the aubergine purée, galangal and enough water to make a sauce. Simmer until the vegetables are just cooked.

At the last minute, stir in the fresh mint and sweet basil leaves with salt to taste. Serve with noodles and Crunchy Sweet-and-Sour Salad (page 126).

CRUNCHY SWEET-AND-SOUR SALAD

SERVES 4–6

⅓ small head of Chinese leaves,
   thinly sliced
bunch of watercress
large handful of spinach leaves,
   sliced, or young leaf spinach
200 g/7 oz beansprouts
85 g/3 oz mange-tout peas, cut into
   strips lengthwise
4 spring onions, cut into strips
85 g/3 oz skinned shelled peanuts,
   dry-roasted in a pan and crushed

small handful of fresh mint
small handful of sweet basil leaves

For the dressing
2 tablespoons oil
3 garlic cloves, sliced
2 tablespoons lime juice
2 tablespoons light soy sauce
1 dessertspoon brown sugar or
   honey
2 red chillies, thinly sliced

Crunchy Sweet-and-Sour Salad is another of the dishes we sampled at the wedding, sitting on the floor among a hundred happy people, with most of whom we didn't share a word of language.

Mix the Chinese leaves, watercress, spinach, beansprouts and mange-tout peas in a bowl.

Make the dressing: in a heavy-based pan heat the oil and fry the garlic until brown and crunchy. Remove the pan from heat and add the lime juice, soy sauce, brown sugar or honey and the chillies. Stir until all ingredients are combined. Allow to cool slightly, then pour over the salad.

Finally, sprinkle the spring onions, peanuts and herbs on top.

Left **Detail from a Buddhist temple in Vientiane**
Right **Crunchy Sweet-and-Sour Salad**

THAILAND

Thailand is one of the easy countries of Asia for foreign tourists. It has an abundance of natural beauty, from the jungly hills of the north to the forests and rivers of the centre and the tropical paradises of the southern peninsula. Visitors can explore the spectacular ruins of past Siamese kingdoms and colourful living temples, ride an elephant or trek to a tribal village in the hills, and enjoy idyllic beaches, bargain-shopping, great-value accommodation and efficient public transport. The country has developed a massive tourist industry, the downside of which is that it is all too easy to spend a trip almost entirely in the company of other tourists. Thailand demands so little in return for all it offers that travelling there almost seems like cheating.

Despite providing such a generous holiday destination, Thais have kept much of the traditional grace and elegance of their way of life, together with a unique cuisine. Never having been invaded or colonized (a singular history in southern Asia), they have food that is undiluted Thai and very good. Fresh ingredients are cooked in heavily spiced pastes and flavoured with lemon grass, lime leaves, galangal root, black pepper, sweet basil, ginger, tamarind, coconut milk, peanuts and coriander leaves. Being completely vegetarian can be complicated by the fish and shrimp sauces that are much used in Thai cooking, but these can easily be excluded when cooking at home. Anyone who enjoys eating fish and seafood will be well satisfied, especially in southern Thailand. There are some excellent vegetarian restaurants in Bangkok and in larger towns such as Chiang Mai. Some are smart and relatively expensive; others, including those set up by the Theravada Buddhists, indicated by a large green sign with a Thai numeral on it, are incredibly cheap.

One of our first experiences of travel in Asia was several weeks spent living for a few pence a night in palm-thatched beach-huts on various islands in the Gulf of Thailand. Our budget was so tight that we didn't want to use any of it buying the food on sale in the tourist cafés along the beach, so we cooked every night on a paraffin stove outside our hut, using whatever we found in the local market. We didn't know much about Thai cooking at the time, but simply enjoyed experimenting with all the ingredients we came across. Since then we have learnt far more about how to use these ingredients to create more traditional and much tastier Thai dishes.

A huge statue of the Buddha in the ruins of Sukhothai, the ancient Siamese capital

This stir-fry is a dish we ate on the street in Bangkok after watching a film in an open-air street cinema. The film was projected on to a sheet suspended between two trees. It cost a few bhat to sit in front of the trees, while to watch the film back to front behind the sheet was free. Both sides of the sheet drew large crowds, as did the street-food stalls which produced this feast in just a few minutes.

BANGKOK STIR-FRY

Serves 4

4 tablespoons sunflower oil
8 baby aubergines, cut into quarters lengthwise
salt
300 g/10 oz deep-fried tofu, cut into 1 cm/½ inch slices

225 g/8 oz fine green beans
4 fresh red chillies, cut into strips
good pinch of crushed dried red chilli
2 teaspoons brown sugar
400 ml/14 fl oz coconut milk
handful of chopped coriander leaves

Make sure you have all ingredients prepared and at hand ready to throw in.

Heat the sunflower oil in a wok. When hot, fry the aubergine, sprinkled with a little salt to avoid it absorbing too much oil and drying out, until the aubergine starts to soften.

Add the tofu and the green beans and flash-fry for a few minutes. Add the fresh chillies, the crushed chillies and the brown sugar, stirring constantly to avoid sticking.

Reduce the heat and add the coconut milk. Simmer for 5 minutes. Season with salt to taste. Serve with noodles and garnished with coriander leaves.

JUNGLE CURRY

This curry is made with a red curry paste that can be made in advance and stored in the fridge.

SERVES 4–6

4 tablespoons sunflower oil

150 g/5 oz baby sweetcorn, cut down the middle lengthwise

2 small red peppers, deseeded and thinly sliced

225 g/8 oz green beans, cut in half

225 g/8 oz button mushrooms, cut in half

2 small heads of broccoli, broken into florets

350 ml/12 fl oz stock

1 tablespoon dark soy sauce

4 kaffir lime leaves, rolled and thinly sliced

1 dessertspoon brown sugar

salt

For the red curry paste

4 hot red chillies

4 garlic cloves

2 lemon grass stalks, thinly sliced

5 cm/2 inch cube of galangal or ginger, peeled and chopped

1 red onion, roughly chopped

½ teaspoon salt

1 dessertspoon coriander seeds, dry-roasted and ground

For the garnish

coriander leaves, chopped

red chillies, thinly sliced

First make the red curry paste simply by blending all ingredients in a food processor.

Heat the sunflower oil in a wok and, when it is hot, add the red curry paste. Fry for a few seconds, stirring constantly. Now add the vegetables, still stirring constantly until they are well coated with the paste and starting to soften.

Pour over the stock and the soy sauce. Add the lime leaves and sugar. Simmer until the vegetables are just soft but retain a little bite, adding more water if necessary.

Finally add salt to taste. Garnish with chopped coriander leaves and thinly sliced red chillies. Serve with rice or noodles and Beancurd and Beansprout Spicy Salad (page 133).

'Jungle curries', from the northern part of Thailand, are characterized by strong flavours and the absence of the sweet coconut milk so favoured in the south. The most memorable jungle curry we tasted was one that we ate while staying in a forest guest-house among the great Buddha statues that are scattered around the ruins of Sukhothai.

Jungle Curry

THAI GREEN CURRY

SERVES 4–6

4 tablespoons sunflower oil

6 baby aubergines, cut into quarters, or 8 Thai aubergines, cut in half

⅔ head of a medium cauliflower, cut into small florets

150 g/5 oz fine green beans, cut in half

175 g/6 oz oyster mushrooms, sliced

150 ml/¼ pint stock

4 kaffir lime leaves, rolled up and thinly sliced

2 dessertspoons dark soy sauce

1 dessertspoon brown sugar

400 ml/14 fl oz coconut milk

large handful of sweet basil leaves

salt

chopped coriander leaves, to garnish

For the green curry paste

1 teaspoon coriander seeds

1 teaspoon cumin seeds

1 dessertspoon black peppercorns

large handful of coriander stalks, chopped

6 shallots or 1 red onion, coarsely chopped

4 garlic cloves

5 cm/2 inch cube of galangal or root ginger, peeled and roughly chopped

2 lemon grass stalks, thinly sliced

4 green chillies

1 tablespoon dark soy sauce (or 1 teaspoon fish sauce)

grated zest and juice of 1 lime

Thai Green Curry with its aromatic coconut milk sauce is typical of the south, and is our favourite Thai curry. It is actually not very green, but most of the ingredients of the paste that forms the basis of the curry are. You can use almost any vegetable, but aubergine works particularly well. If you can get small round Thai aubergines, all the better; baby aubergines are a good substitute and are available from most good supermarkets.

First make the green curry paste: dry-roast the coriander and cumin seeds in a small pan, then mix them with the peppercorns and grind using a spice grinder or pestle and mortar. Add to a food processor with all remaining ingredients and process until a paste forms. Store in the fridge if making in advance.

Heat the sunflower oil in a wok. When hot, fry the aubergines (sprinkled with a little salt to prevent them absorbing all the oil and drying up too much) until it starts to soften. Add the cauliflower, green beans and oyster mushrooms.

When the cauliflower starts to brown, add the green curry paste, stirring well to avoid sticking. When this is well combined, add the stock, kaffir lime leaves, dark soy sauce and sugar. When the vegetables are just starting to soften, add the coconut milk and sweet basil. Cook for a further 5 minutes, ensuring the sauce doesn't boil. Season with salt to taste, if necessary.

Serve with rice or noodles, garnished with chopped coriander leaves.

Fried beancurd (tofu) makes a lovely side-dish to be served with any of the Thai curries in this chapter. Deep-fried tofu can be bought from any health-food or oriental shop, or from good supermarkets – much easier than frying it yourself.

The Buddha's hand — a detail from one of the statues around the ruins of Sukhothai

BEANCURD AND BEANSPROUT SPICY SALAD

Serves 4–6

1 cucumber, grated
1 red pepper, cut into fine strips
200 g/7 oz beansprouts
300 g/10 oz deep-fried tofu, cut into 1 cm/½ inch slices
1 tablespoon sunflower oil
1 garlic clove, crushed
1–2 green chillies, thinly sliced
1–2 red chillies, thinly sliced

juice of 1 lime
2 tablespoons light soy sauce
1 dessertspoon brown sugar or honey
125 g/4 oz skinned shelled peanuts, dry-roasted in a pan and then crushed
handful of coriander leaves, chopped

Combine the grated cucumber, red pepper and beansprouts in a salad bowl.

Fry the tofu slices in hot oil until they are brown and crunchy. Place to one side and allow to cool.

Using the same pan, fry the garlic and chillies for a few seconds, then add the lime juice, soy sauce and brown sugar or honey. Stir until all these dressing ingredients are combined.

Arrange the fried tofu slices on top of the salad, sprinkle with the crushed peanuts, pour on the dressing and garnish with lots of coriander leaves.

MALAYSIA & INDONESIA

Peninsular Malaysia, Borneo and all the Indonesian islands share an essentially common language and cuisine. The language, Bahasa, is very easy to learn, and with little variation the spoken language is understood all the way from the air-conditioned office blocks of Kuala Lumpur and Jakarta to the most remote longhouse in the jungles of Sarawak or Irian Jaya. Numerous regional languages, and Chinese dialects and Tamil, are spoken through the region, but a knowledge of Bahasa will enable a tourist to communicate with most people, most of the time.

As far as food is concerned there are regional variations too, and rather more of a difference between Malaysia and Indonesia than with language. The ingredients themselves remain more constant. Vegetarian food is easy to find. A street food classic is the delicious satay sauce made from roasted peanuts blended with spices, into which barbecued chicken or red meat is usually dipped. Luckily for vegetarians, a raw vegetable and beancurd dish, gado gado (page 143), served with a similar sauce, is common throughout Indonesia. There are also numerous fried rice, beancurd and egg dishes, as well as vegetable concoctions in coconut milk curries, to choose from.

Peninsular Malaysia, like Thailand, is so undemanding of the tourist that it makes for a perfect holiday destination. The east coast is less developed than the richer, more urban west; some of the offshore islands are sensationally beautiful, and a train journey from Gemas to Kota Bharu through the centre passes through some impressive rainforest. My real jungle experience came on a Royal Geographical Society assignment to the Batu Apoi Forest Reserve in the remote Temburong district of eastern Brunei on the island of Borneo. Thanks to its phenomenal oil wealth, Brunei's tropical rainforests have largely escaped felling for profit. In this, as in much else, it differs sharply from the rest of Borneo.

To reach the reserve I had to travel from the capital, down the Brunei River, across open sea, through mangrove swamps and up the Temburong River to the sleepy settlement of Bangar. A Land Rover then took me cross-country to an Iban longhouse at Batang Duri on the Kuala (river) Belalong. From here the journey was by motorized canoe, negotiating rocks and rapids all the way up to the riverside jungle clearing where a collection of wooden huts on stilts was to be home for the next six weeks.

A highlight of my trip was a four-day trek to Bukit Belalong, the topmost point in the reserve. Sleeping out in the forest on stretchers suspended above the forest floor, so as to escape the worst of the leeches, was much more cosy than I had imagined it

The dense rainforest of the remote Batu Apoi Forest Reserve

would be. Bed was the only place to be dry, and we carefully preserved a spare set of dry clothes to sleep in, changing back into our damp daytime clothing in the morning. There was no point in trying to stay dry: within seconds of setting off into the forest, perspiration and damp from the regular rainfall soaked everything. Putting on wet clothes isn't the most pleasant way to start a day — but the dawn chorus of gibbon calls above the mutterings of a million birds and insects made up for a lot. In fact, I have found that one way of conveying how amazing it is to be in the rainforest is to relate the hardships — which include constant thirst, complete exhaustion, fear of getting lost (and dying), sliding painfully down steep muddy banks, and finding leeches in one's underclothes. For, despite all this, it is still an unforgettable experience in an entirely positive way.

SPICY GARLIC-FRIED GREEN VEGETABLES

Black bean paste, made from soya beans, is available at most supermarkets or oriental stores; if you can't find it, simply use finely chopped salted black soya beans.

SERVES 4–6

- 4 tablespoons sunflower oil
- 8 shallots or 2 red onions, thinly sliced
- 4 garlic cloves, sliced
- 4 red chillies, thinly sliced
- 4 small courgettes, cut into fat matchsticks
- 150 g/5 oz okra, cut in half lengthwise
- 200 g/7 oz sugar snap peas
- 1 small head of Chinese leaves, cut into 2.5 cm/1 inch slices
- 250 g/9 oz spinach, shredded
- 2 tablespoons black bean paste (or 1 tablespoon salted black beans, finely chopped and mixed with 1 tablespoon water)
- 2 tablespoons brown sugar or honey
- 2 tablespoons dark soy sauce

Heat the oil in a wok and, when hot, stir-fry the shallots or onions, garlic and chillies.

Add the courgettes, okra, sugar snap peas and Chinese leaves, stirring constantly. When the vegetables start to soften, throw in the spinach and when it starts to wilt add the black bean paste or chopped salted black beans, the brown sugar or honey and the soy sauce. Stir well.

Finally add 5 tablespoons of water to help soften the vegetables and fry until all the ingredients are well combined. Serve immediately.

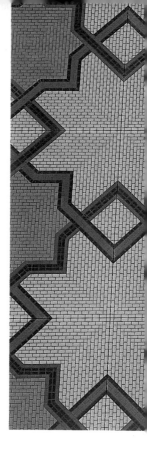

We watched these spicy garlic-fried green vegetables being cooked in front of our eyes at a stall in a Singapore food market. As with most stir-fries, the recipe relies on a hot wok and all the ingredients being at hand ready to throw in. It can be served as a side-dish or as a full meal.

MALAYSIAN FRUIT AND VEGETABLE SALAD

SERVES 4–6

1 small firm mango, peeled and
  cubed

1 firm pear, cored and cubed

½ pineapple, peeled, cored and
  cubed

2 carrots, cubed

125g/4 oz beansprouts

1 red pepper, deseeded and cut into
  thin slices

1 tablespoon crushed roasted
  skinned peanuts, for garnish

handful of coriander leaves,
  chopped, for garnish

For the dressing

2 tablespoons light soy sauce

2 teaspoons honey or brown sugar

1 red chilli, finely chopped

1 tablespoon tamarind paste

juice of 1 lime

Combine all the vegetable and fruit salad ingredients in a salad bowl.

Make the dressing by simply combining all the ingredients with 2
tablespoons of water until the sugar has dissolved.

Pour the dressing over the salad and sprinkle with crushed peanuts and
chopped coriander leaves to serve.

MALAY SAMBAL

SERVES 4–6

2 small red onions, roughly chopped
4 garlic cloves
4 red chillies
45 g / 1½ oz ground almonds
2 lemon grass stalks, thinly sliced
5 cm / 2 inch cube of galangal or
   root ginger, peeled and chopped
400 g / 14 oz tomatoes, roughly
   chopped
4 tablespoons sunflower oil
2 medium sweet potatoes, cubed
4 carrots, cut into matchsticks
½ small white cabbage, finely
   shredded
200 g / 7 oz baby sweetcorn, halved
   lengthwise
bunch of spring onions, cut into
   2.5 cm / 1 inch strips

4 kaffir lime leaves, rolled up and
   thinly sliced
200 ml / 7 fl oz coconut milk
1 generous dessertspoon sugar or
   honey
juice of 1 lime
salt

For the garnish
125 g / 4 oz beansprouts
⅓ cucumber, grated
2 red chillies, thinly sliced
   lengthwise
handful of coriander leaves, chopped
good shake of soy sauce
juice of 1 lime
60 g / 2 oz crushed roast peanuts

The island of Tioman on Malaysia's east coast can be reached by fishing boat from Mersing. From the jetty a footpath climbs into the rainforest, past giant monitor lizards and waterfalls, over a ridge, then steeply down to the refreshingly clear water of the South China Sea at Kampung Juara. We stayed here, sleeping a few metres from the sea in a simple A-frame hut and eating each day in one of the two beach cafés, where we discovered the Malay sambal dish that we describe here.

In a food processor, blend the red onion, garlic, chillies, ground almonds, lemon grass, galangal and tomatoes. Set aside.

Heat the sunflower oil in a wok and, when hot, fry the sweet potato until it starts to brown. Add the carrots and fry for a few minutes. Then add the cabbage and fry until it starts to wilt.

Add the corn and spring onions with the lime leaves and the spice / tomato mixture. Stir until the vegetables are coated. Add enough water to make a thickish sauce and gently simmer until the vegetables are just soft but retain some bite.

Add the coconut milk, sugar and lime juice, with salt to taste. Simmer for a further minute or two. The sambal is now ready to serve.

Garnish with the mixed beansprouts, cucumber, chilli, coriander, soy sauce, lime juice and crushed peanuts. Serve with rice.

KUCHING TAMARIND AND COCONUT MILK CURRY

This curry, which is very popular across southern Malaysia and Kuching, works particularly well with noodles.

SERVES 4–6

1 red onion or 6 shallots, roughly chopped

3 garlic cloves

4 red chillies

2 teaspoons tamarind paste

1 tablespoon dark soy sauce

scant ½ teaspoon ground turmeric

4 tablespoons sunflower oil

6 baby aubergines, cut into quarters

salt

½ small white cabbage, finely shredded

1 large red pepper, thinly sliced

300 g / 10 oz pak choy, roughly broken up

400 ml / 14 fl oz coconut milk

200 g / 7 oz beansprouts

To garnish

2 shallots, thinly sliced

large handful of coriander leaves, chopped

2 red chillies, thinly sliced

Chinese characters on a shop front in Malaysia

Whizz the onion, garlic, chilli, tamarind paste, soy sauce and turmeric in a food processor until they form a paste.

Heat the sunflower oil in a wok and, when hot, fry the baby aubergine, sprinkled with a little salt to prevent it from absorbing too much oil.

Add the flavouring paste and stir well until the aubergine is coated with it. Add the shredded cabbage and sliced red pepper, stirring constantly. Pour on some water to loosen the spices and make a sauce. Cook until the vegetables are tender but not too soft.

Add the pak choy, coconut milk and beansprouts. Simmer for a further 3 minutes, but do not allow to boil. If necessary, add salt to taste.

Serve in bowls with a generous garnish of thinly sliced shallots, chopped coriander leaves and thinly sliced red chillies.

BORNEO RAINFOREST VEGETABLES

SERVES 4–6

1 teaspoon ground coriander seeds

1 teaspoon crushed dried red chillies

1 teaspoon ground turmeric

2 teaspoons ground almonds

1 large onion

4 garlic cloves

3 tablespoons sunflower oil

300 g/10 oz tempeh, cut into strips

3 tablespoons cashew nuts

1 lemon grass stalk, cut into short lengths and bruised

5 cm/2 inch piece of galangal, chopped and bruised

200 g/7 oz baby sweetcorn, halved lengthwise

200 g/7 oz cauliflower florets

200 g/7 oz green beans, cut in half lengthwise

1 can (400 g/14 oz) of coconut milk

1 tablespoon coconut milk powder, mixed to a paste with water

For the garnish

thin strips of fresh red chilli

coriander leaves

roasted peanuts

In a food processor, blend the coriander, chillies, turmeric, almonds, onion and garlic to a paste.

Heat the oil in a heavy pan and fry the tempeh and cashew nuts until they turn brown. Add the garlic paste, the lemon grass and the galangal, and cook for 2 minutes.

Add all the vegetables and toss to coat in the paste. Add the coconut milk and simmer until the vegetables are soft.

Remove the lemon grass and galangal, and stir in the coconut milk paste to thicken.

Serve with rice, garnished with thin strips of fresh red chilli, coriander leaves and roasted peanuts.

One of the most pleasant surprises during my stay at the Batu Apoi Forest Reserve in Brunei was the presence of two excellent and entertaining Indonesian cooks; another was the location of an Iban 'short house' on the edge of the camp to accommodate the Iban guides and porters. Between cooking and language lessons and Iban hospitality there was never a dull evening. By day the rainforest, awesome in its scale and mystery, provided countless photographic delights and an unparalleled feeling of disregard for anything that might exist beyond it. This tempeh and cashew-nut dish that I ate there is one of the best reminders of that time.

Borneo Rainforest Vegetables

BALINESE GADO GADO

SERVES 4–6

3 carrots, cut into matchstick strips
200 g/7 oz beansprouts
125 g/4 oz fine green beans
125 g/4 oz sugar snap peas
½ cucumber, cut into thickish
matchstick strips
1 small head of Chinese leaves,
thinly sliced

For the peanut sauce
1 large red onion, coarsely chopped
3 garlic cloves
3 fresh red chillies
175 g/6 oz skinned peanuts
2 tablespoons sunflower oil
1 tablespoon soy sauce
1 dessertspoon tamarind paste,
dissolved in 2 tablespoons water

150 ml/¼ pint coconut milk
1 tablespoon smooth peanut butter
1 dessertspoon brown sugar
2 lemon grass stalks, cut down the
middle and bashed with a rolling
pin
salt

For the garnish
4 hard-boiled eggs, cut into wedges
4 tomatoes, cut into wedges
200 g/7 oz tempeh, cut into strips
and fried (if not available use
1 cm/½ inch slices of deep-fried
tofu, fried until crunchy)
large handful of spinach, shredded
1 large onion, dry-fried (page 145)
handful of coriander leaves, chopped

First make the sauce: blend the onion, garlic and chillies in a food processor until they form a paste. Gently dry-roast the peanuts in a pan, stirring to avoid burning. Allow to cool, and crush them in a food processor until finely ground. Heat the oil in a wok. When hot, add the onion paste and fry, stirring constantly, for a minute. Add the ground peanuts and stir until all the ingredients are combined. Add the soy sauce, tamarind, coconut milk, peanut butter, sugar and lemon grass. Gently cook until all the flavours are combined and a thickish sauce has formed (add a little water if necessary). Finally, take out the lemon grass and season with salt to taste.

Combine all the salad ingredients (you can serve this dish either in individual portions or in one big bowl). Pour the warm sauce over the salad, then arrange the egg, tomato, tempeh or tofu around the edge and pile the spinach and dry-fried onions in the centre. Sprinkle with coriander leaves.

We loved Bali: the food was excellent, the people graceful and friendly, the temples fascinating and the landscapes enchanting. It was refreshing to see a place where mass tourism has been managed so well, maintaining most of the dignity and traditions of the local culture while providing comfortable accommodation and such good food for visitors. We did not see the whole island and there may well be places where this equation has not been so convincing, but for us Bali was travelling at its best.

Our favourite beachside lunch in Bali, gado gado is an unusual combination of hot and cold ingredients. The cooked peanut sauce is poured over a crunchy salad, which is served with hard-boiled eggs and dry-fried onions.

Balinese Gado Gado

TEMPEH GORENG AND BEANSPROUTS

Serves 4–6

4 garlic cloves, crushed

1 teaspoon ground coriander seeds

225 g/8 oz tempeh, cut into chunky sticks

4 tablespoons sunflower oil

200 g/7 oz beansprouts

3 tablespoons soy sauce

Mix the crushed garlic and coriander with 2 tablespoons water to make a paste.

Fry the tempeh sticks in the oil until brown, moving them around gently. Then add the garlic paste. After 30 seconds, add the beansprouts. Mix well, add the soy sauce and serve.

Tempeh goreng is real bus-station food. In Bali, even in small towns, bus stations encourage fast-food street stalls. At night they are entertaining, even romantic places to eat, all lit up and full of animated bustle. By day, however, the illusion is swiftly shattered by the number of flies and the state of the kitchens.

144

The thin, spicy sauces known as sambals form part of most meals in Malaysia and Indonesia.

Usually a table will be laid with sambals and a variety of other accompaniments, all served in small dishes. We list a few suggestions here:
Dry-fried onions (thinly sliced and gently fried in a hot dry pan until brown)
Thinly sliced red onions
Sliced chillies
Sliced spring onions
Crushed roasted peanuts
Prawn crackers
Sliced cucumber
Grated coconut
Tempeh, broken up into individual grains, then fried in oil until brown.

MALAYSIAN SAMBAL

SERVES 4–6

2 green chillies, finely chopped
2 red chillies, finely chopped
2 spring onions, finely chopped
½ teaspoon salt

juice of 1 lime
2 teaspoons honey or brown sugar
1 tablespoon cider vinegar

Mix all the ingredients together and allow to stand for 15 minutes before serving.

INDONESIAN SAMBAL

SERVES 4–6

2 garlic cloves, very finely chopped
2 red chillies, finely chopped
juice of ½ lime

1 teaspoon sugar or honey
2 tablespoons dark soy sauce

Mix all the ingredients together and allow to stand for 15 minutes before serving.

The Americas

The Americas

In every country we visited between the Rio Grande of Mexico and Rio de Janeiro in Brazil we ate beans and rice in one form or another. There are many regional variations in the way beans and rice, the ubiquitous staple foods, are served, and this chapter includes some of the most delicious. Other dishes — especially vegetarian ones — did sometimes prove rather hard to track down. Brazil and Mexico offered the most interesting variety: here we found lots of exciting fresh fruits and vegetables and cheeses, with spicy sauces and salsas. In the Andean countries we found stews of sweetcorn and squashes, while in Costa Rica the beans and rice were punctuated with salads and Caribbean tastes such as plantain and coconut milk. In Cuba it was sometimes a problem to find anything to eat at all.

To some extent, cities such as Rio de Janeiro, La Paz, Lima and Quito are European in flavour. The Hispanic or Portuguese colonial centres have been surrounded by the type of modern development common to most Western cities. However, on the outskirts of large cities shanty towns and *favelas* are swollen by the exodus of rural poor joining the deprived urban underclass. The affluent city élite is more likely to be descended from colonial stock rather than from indigenous South Americans. It is easy (if somewhat expensive) to stay in such cities eating only in the restaurants of the privileged, and it can be rather dangerous as

a foreigner to venture too far from comfortable familiarity into the twilight zones of raw street-life.

Beyond the cities there are better opportunities to gain experiences of culture and people outside the European traditions. In the rainforests of the Brazilian Amazon, on the high altiplano of the Andes and in the coastal deserts of Peru we travelled through some stunning landscapes and met plenty of indigenous people, ranging from tribal forest Indians to Quechua-speaking mountain *campesinos*. However, I have to confess that in South America all the best food we discovered was in the comfortable restaurants and homes of the city élite. Nonetheless, despite their evident European influences, all the recipes we have chosen owe as much to their South American home as to any colonial past.

In Central America and Mexico our experience was notably different, and some of the best meals we had were in roadside, beachside and jungle cafés, far from the comforts of any city.

Pages 146–147 **Sunset over Rio de Janeiro**

Above **A tortilla is deftly filled with cheese at a street stall in Oaxaca, Mexico.**
Left **A woman leads her llama through the streets of Cuzco, Peru.**

BRAZIL

The first time I visited Brazil was for a Royal Geographical Society project in the far north-east, on a remote island called Ilha de Maraca. The island, surrounded by tributaries of the Rio Branco, is covered in dense rainforest. Trails were being cut with machetes by local guides to facilitate the team of scientists due to arrive; I was to photograph the environment in its original state before research began. Apart from the trails, dugout canoes provided the only way of getting around. My second trip to the rainforest was less demanding. In the Itatiaia Reserve between Rio de Janeiro and São Paulo the hilly terrain gives better views of the forest, which reveals itself as full of waterfalls and butterflies, and is much easier to get to.

Brazilians love to eat meat and some restaurants serve nothing but meat, by the plateful. However, there is no shortage of excellent vegetarian restaurants in most Brazilian cities. Many are open only at lunchtime and serve fixed-price buffet meals, including selections of fresh salads, fruity salsas and adaptations of traditional dishes. The cosmopolitan nature of Rio has encouraged a more eclectic choice of ingredients than is found anywhere else in South America.

A view of the Amazon
jungle in the rain

On my first day in the rainforest, downriver with one of the guides in a canoe, we misjudged some rapids and knocked the outboard motor out of action. With 20 km (12 miles) of uncut jungle between us and the camp, and piranhas in the water, I felt a very long way from home. Eventually the guide managed to fix the motor with his machete, and we made it back to base thankful to have avoided a twenty-day hack though the forest.

That night the wives of the guides cooked a huge pot of stew for everyone in the camp, a version of the dish cozido (which usually contains pork and sausages), using mounds of fresh vegetables that we had brought with us from Boa Vista.

COZIDO

SERVES 4–6

300 g/10 oz 'Buddhist meat' or
    deep-fried tofu, sliced
350 g/12 oz (prepared weight)
    pumpkin, peeled, deseeded and
    cubed
5 tablespoons olive oil
1 plantain, cut into 1 cm/½ inch slices
125 g/4 oz okra, sliced lengthwise
1 onion, thinly sliced
2 garlic cloves, crushed
1 heaped teaspoon coriander seeds,
    crushed
2 small turnips, cubed
225 g/8 oz hard white cabbage, cubed
300 g/10 oz marrow, peeled
    and deseeded, cut into

2.5 cm/1 inch cubes
300 g/10 oz sweet potatoes, cut
    into 2.5 cm/1 inch cubes
300 ml/½ pint stock
handful of fresh parsley, chopped
salt and pepper

For the marinade
2 garlic cloves, crushed
1 teaspoon coriander seeds, crushed
handful of fresh parsley, chopped
1 onion, thinly sliced
1 dessertspoon balsamic vinegar
3 tablespoons tamari or soy sauce
3 bay leaves
1 tablespoon olive oil

Combine the marinade ingredients and pour them over the sliced Buddhist meat or tofu in a bowl. Allow to stand for 1 hour. Pour off the marinade, retaining the liquid, and set the Buddhist meat or tofu to one side.

Meanwhile, cook the pumpkin in boiling salted water until soft. Drain, retaining the pumpkin water. Mash the pumpkin and set aside.

Heat half the oil in a large pan, add the sliced plantain and fry until browned. Remove from pan. Add the marinated Buddhist meat or tofu and the okra, and fry until both are browned. Remove from pan. Heat the remaining oil and add the onion and garlic. When these begin to soften, add the crushed coriander seeds. Stir and add the turnip, cabbage, marrow and sweet potato. Stir to coat the vegetables in the oil and coriander. Add the stock, 300 ml/½ pint of the reserved pumpkin water and the reserved marinade. Simmer until the vegetables are soft.

Stir in the mashed pumpkin, then add the fried Buddhist meat or tofu, the okra and the plantain. Simmer gently for a few minutes to allow the flavours to infuse. Add the parsley and season to taste. Serve with rice.

BLACK BEAN STEW

SERVES 4–6

250 g/9 oz black turtle beans,
     soaked overnight in cold water
1 large red onion, diced
4 garlic cloves, crushed
3 red chillies, finely chopped
2 tablespoons olive oil
30 g/1 oz butter
450 g/1 lb sweet potatoes, cubed
225 g/8 oz turnips, cubed

2 carrots, cubed
1 red pepper, deseeded and cubed
250 g/9 oz tomatoes, finely diced
150 ml/¼ pint stock
2 large handfuls of coriander,
     chopped, plus more to garnish
handful of parsley, finely chopped
2 bay leaves
salt and pepper

Drain the black beans, place in a saucepan and cover with water. Bring to the boil, then simmer, with the lid on, until the beans are soft.

Meanwhile, fry the onion, garlic and chilli in the olive oil until soft. Remove one-third of the soft black beans and their cooking liquid, and add this to the fried onion. Mash the onion and beans with a potato masher, until the beans start to break down. Return to remaining beans and cooking liquid.

Melt the butter in a large pan, add the sweet potato, turnip, carrot and red pepper, and fry until they start to soften. Add the chopped tomato and fry until the tomato breaks down. Add the black beans and their broth, the stock, coriander, parsley and bay leaves. Simmer until vegetables are soft and the flavours combined. Season with salt and pepper to taste.

MANGO SALSA

SERVES 4–6

1 large ripe mango, peeled and cubed
2 small carrots, diced
2 celery stalks, diced
1 orange, peeled and cut into cubes

1 green chilli, finely chopped
handful of coriander, chopped
juice of 1 lime
pepper

Combine all the ingredients, season with pepper to taste and chill for about 30 minutes before serving.

This colourful black bean recipe is an adaptation of a traditional Brazilian dish. When it is served with mango salsa, the bright reds and yellows contrast strikingly with the black turtle beans.

Black Bean Stew

BOLIVIA

La Paz is the highest capital city in the world, and my arrival there was a dramatic one. By a twist of fate, having nearly missed the flight from Santa Cruz, I had been invited to fly in the last remaining seat — in the cockpit with the pilot. The view of the Andes rising out of the Amazon Basin, as seen through the windscreen of a 737, was an incredible novelty. As the aeroplane passed over the snowy peaks in the half-light of dusk they seemed only a hundred metres below us; beyond them, La Paz came into view, a bowl of lights sunk in the dark expanse of the altiplano. We descended through

Shadowy figures in the
La Paz fog

shafts of lightning from an electrical storm to a runway 3,660 metres (12,000 ft) above sea level. The air is cold and thin at this altitude. The effort of carrying my bags up to a third-floor hotel room was exhausting and my sleep full of nightmares.

Bolivia was in the midst of its own nightmare, an economic one. Inflation was running at 45,000 per cent. The exchange rate for US dollars rose several times daily, the banks were closed, and on street corners men in leather jackets exchanged pesos by the carrier-bag from tea-chests full of notes. A cup of coffee cost two million pesos; eating out meant taking along a bag of money to pay the bill. For the first time in my life I was a millionaire. La Paz was a city of millionaires, many of them desperately poor.

SWEETCORN STEW

SERVES 4–6

3 carrots, diced

3 medium potatoes, peeled and diced

4 tablespoons sunflower oil

2 onions, finely chopped

4 garlic cloves, crushed

1 jalapeño chilli, finely chopped

2 large ripe plum tomatoes, cubed

1 tablespoon sweet paprika

1 handful of fresh oregano, chopped

1 handful of fresh parsley, chopped

3 large handfuls of spinach, finely shredded

4 sweetcorn cobs, cut into rounds about 2.5 cm / 1 inch thick and parboiled

600 ml / 1 pint stock

salt and pepper

handful of coriander leaves, chopped, to garnish

Bolivia in general is not great for vegetarians. La Paz is. Near the university I found possibly the best vegetarian restaurant in South America. However, the style of food in the vegetarian cafés was as much Californian as Bolivian. The best local dish I ate was a sweetcorn stew we had in a hillside restaurant on the way back from an exhilarating day out on the highest ski-slope in the world.

This is a very tasty way of eating sweetcorn, which takes on all the flavours of the gravy in which it is boiled.

Parboil the carrots and potatoes in salted water until they start to soften.

Heat the oil in saucepan and, when hot, fry the onion, garlic and chilli until soft. Add the tomatoes, paprika, oregano and parsley. Stir well.

Add the parboiled carrots and potatoes with the spinach. Fry, stirring constantly, until the spinach wilts.

Add the sweetcorn and the stock. Cover and simmer until the vegetables are nice and soft. Add salt and pepper to taste, then lightly mash the carrots and potato into the sauce.

Serve garnished with the chopped coriander and accompanied by crusty bread and a leafy green salad.

PERU

The jungles, deserts, mountains and coast of Peru offer an abundance of exciting photographic opportunities, but a dearth of stimulating culinary experiences. Although many of the landscapes are well worth going a little hungry for, when we did find good food it was very welcome.

We entered Peru from Bolivia by ferry across Lake Titicaca in torrential rain. We were travelling through the Andes in midsummer – the wettest time of year. The floating reed islands of the Uros Indians out on the lake were soggy and decaying; the islanders looked bedraggled and unhappy. The only produce in the flooded vegetable market in Puno was rotting coriander. Much of the railway line was under water, but we just managed to catch the last slow train over the altiplano.

Despite the weather, we walked the last day of the Inca Trail up to Machu Picchu, the spectacular 'lost city of the Incas' hidden high in the Urubamba valley. Later, I went back alone to the site at dawn. I climbed the tower of Wayna Picchu and looked down on the deserted city through the swirling clouds from the Temple of the Moon. Machu Picchu stays in my memory as one of the highlights of all my travels.

Dawn in the Andes

POTATO CAKES WITH CUCUMBER RELISH

In Cuzco, better food and accommodation, the colonial splendours of the capital and the dramatic ruins of Inca cities all combined to take our minds off the incessant rain. We ate these fried potato cakes with a vegetable filling and a spicy cucumber relish in the Plaza de Armas, where every evening women set up their stalls.

SERVES 4–6

1 kg/2¼ lb potatoes, peeled and cubed
about 3 tablespoons milk
45 g/1½ oz butter
salt and pepper
2 onions, finely chopped
2 fresh red chillies, finely chopped
4 garlic cloves, crushed
handful of coriander stalks, finely chopped
2 carrots, finely diced

2 red peppers, finely diced
oil for frying

For the cucumber relish
1 large cucumber, grated
2 green chillies, finely chopped
handful of coriander leaves, finely chopped
juice of 1 lemon
2 teaspoons honey
salt

Cook the potatoes in boiling salted water until soft. Drain and mash with a little milk and half the butter until smooth. Season to taste.

Gently melt the remaining butter in a frying pan. Add the onions, red chillies and garlic, and fry until these are soft. Add the coriander stalks, carrots and red pepper, and fry until these are soft.

Now make up the potato cakes: take a handful of the mashed potato, press an indentation into its centre and fill with a little of the carrot and pepper mixture. Work the potato around to seal the stuffing and form into a cake with a diameter of about 7.5 cm/3 inches. Repeat with the remaining potato and filling until all are used up.

Fry the potato cakes in very hot oil in a non-stick frying pan, until golden and crunchy on both sides.

Make the cucumber relish by combining all the ingredients with salt to taste.

Serve the potato cakes with the relish, any of the remaining carrot and pepper mixture and a green leaf salad. Alternatively, they are wonderful with poached eggs.

LIMA BEAN AND PUMPKIN STEW

Serves 4–6

450 g/1 lb potatoes, cubed
450 g/1 lb pumpkin, peeled, deseeded and cubed
salt and pepper
4 tablespoons sunflower oil
2 onions, finely chopped
3 garlic cloves, crushed
1 jalapeño chilli, finely chopped
1 large ripe plum tomato, cubed
handful of fresh thyme, chopped
2 teaspoons ground cumin

175 g/6 oz cooked lima beans or butter beans
85 g/3 oz fresh or frozen peas
85 g/3 oz fresh or frozen sweetcorn kernels
handful of parsley, finely chopped, to garnish
125 g/4 oz feta cheese, crumbled, to serve

Boil the potatoes and pumpkin in a pan of salted water until they begin to soften. Drain and retain the cooking water.

Heat the oil in a saucepan and, when hot, fry the onion, garlic and chilli until soft. Stir in the tomato, thyme and ground cumin. Add the parboiled potato and pumpkin. Cook with a little of the retained water for a couple of minutes.

Add the beans, peas and corn, and cook for a further 10 minutes. Add salt and pepper to taste.

Serve garnished with the chopped parsley and feta cheese on top, accompanied by rice or crusty bread.

In Lima we found relief from the rain that dogged our stay in Peru. The coastal deserts of Peru along the Pacific Ocean are some of the driest places on earth. Lima itself was a tense city with curfews every night.

We were staying with friends, who took us on day-trips into the desert and out for fine meals in the evening. However, we found our most interesting Peruvian meal on a trip to the Cordillera Blanca Mountains. Along the mountain roads women cooked stews on camp-fires. Among the bubbling pots of foul-smelling concoctions we found a woman selling a lima bean and pumpkin stew. It was very good and set us up brilliantly for our trek into the hills.

Lima Bean and Pumpkin Stew

ECUADOR

The best dish we ate in Ecuador was a creamy pumpkin, potato and paprika soup flavoured with thyme and oregano. We were served it while staying on a ranch in the Andean foothills near the small town of Vilcabamba. The ranch was set in idyllic countryside, while Vilcabamba itself seemed like a Wild West town, with saddled horses tied up outside saloons, and drunks fighting in the town square. We saw a more elegant side of Ecuador in Cuenca, with its cathedral and its gleaming barber-shops, well-stocked pharmacies and tidy cafés around the main square.

For us the highlight of Ecuador was the bustling market town of Otavalo, located at the foot of a volcano, and populated by the best-looking, happiest-seeming and most friendly Indians we met in all of South America. The men wore ponchos and wide-brimmed hats, the women attractive hooped skirts and lots of beads. We watched them play a traditional bat-and-ball game in the streets, although both the bat and the ball were so big that hitting the one with the other was almost impossible and most of the game seemed to be spent chasing after missed balls.

PUMPKIN SOUP

SERVES 4–6

3 tablespoons olive oil
1 onion, finely chopped
2 garlic cloves, crushed
1 heaped teaspoon sweet paprika
handful of fresh oregano, chopped
450 g/1 lb peeled and deseeded
    pumpkin, cubed

350 g/12 oz sweet potato, cubed
600 ml/1 pint stock
salt and pepper
150 ml/¼ pint double cream
handful of chopped fresh thyme, to
    garnish

Heat the olive oil in a saucepan and, when hot, fry the onion until golden. Stir in the garlic, paprika and oregano, and fry for 1 minute. Add the pumpkin and sweet potato, and fry until they start to soften.

Add the stock with enough water to cover the vegetables. Bring to the boil, cover and simmer until the vegetables are soft. Add salt and pepper to taste.

In a blender or food processor, blend the contents of the pan until smooth. Stir in the cream and serve garnished with chopped thyme.

Along the outside of the Catholic cathedral in Cuenca the walls are full of carved effigies in tiny alcoves.

COSTA RICA

More than a quarter of Costa Rica is protected natural wilderness. The country's active policy of conservation, and the immense biodiversity afforded by its tropical location, have allowed 'eco-tourism' to thrive. Areas of rainforest have been developed for visitors in a range of low-impact facilities, from campsites to the so-called 'five-star rustic' resorts that offer a taste of the wildness of nature – but in comfort. This sounded seductive yet improbable, so we set out to discover just how 'five-star' rustic can be, heading into the deep south where there are several remote resorts.

We decided to try the Tiskita Jungle Lodge, situated in 100 hectares (250 acres) of virgin rainforest on the Pacific coast. Our accommodation consisted of a wooden cabin in the forest, with an outdoor bathroom and a wide platform veranda looking out over the treetops and the ocean. The meals, eaten in the communal open-sided dining-room, were excellent. The place was definitely more rustic than five-star, but quite comfortable and friendly. However, communing with nature does include sharing your bedroom with a lot more biodiversity than you'd ever expect in a hotel room – including, one night, an alarmingly large scorpion.

The daytime paradise easily made up for any nocturnal horrors. Troupes of monkeys and parades of exotic birds and eccentric insects provided hours of entertainment as we sat on our veranda. But the real adventures were the forest walks. The trails were clear enough for us to wander off on our own and admire the giant plants, the towering, liana-draped trees, the minute psychedelic-coloured frogs around the forest pools, and a boa constrictor wrapped around a branch. Everywhere the sounds of the forest were incredible: unseen insects created an unruly racket, monkeys whooped and chattered, and birdsong filled the canopy.

Another attraction of Tiskita was experimental fruit orchard walks, on which we were urged to sample extraordinary offerings from a variety of trees. And there was yet more walking to enjoy along the miles of deserted, black sand, palm-fringed beach, with the welcome relief of the foaming Pacific on hand. The rainforest comes right down to the ocean, and here, looking back up at the vastness of the green forest or gazing out across the endless blue sea, we truly appreciated the blissful remoteness of our position; and, as a pair of toucans glided overhead, the privilege of experiencing nature so unspoilt.

One of the beautiful, untouched beaches of Costa Rica's Pacific coast

CRUNCHY SALAD WITH LIME JUICE

Serves 4–6

150 g/5 oz white cabbage, shredded
85 g/3 oz cucumber, diced
1 ripe mango, peeled and diced
1 red pepper, deseeded and diced
6 spring onions, thinly sliced
1 avocado pear, peeled, stoned and cubed

2 handfuls of watercress
juice of 2 limes
1 garlic clove, crushed
3 tablespoons olive oil
salt and pepper

This fresh-tasting salad, with its sweet-and-sour mixture of fruit and vegetables, is typical of the dishes we sampled on the Pacific coast of Costa Rica.

Combine all the ingredients, season to taste and mix well. Chill for about 30 minutes before serving.

A short flight away on the Caribbean side of Costa Rica we found a very different coast and equally different cuisine. The recipe given here is a delicious mixture of sweet potato, pumpkin and plantains in a rich mustard, coconut and rum sauce.

Left **Crunchy Salad with Lime Juice**
Below **Caribbean Vegetables in a Mustard, Coconut and Rum Sauce**

CARIBBEAN VEGETABLES IN A MUSTARD, COCONUT AND RUM SAUCE

2 onions, finely diced
4 garlic cloves
5 cm/2 inch piece of root ginger, peeled and roughly chopped
2 teaspoons coriander seeds
½ teaspoon cloves
5 cm/2 inch piece of cinnamon stick
½ teaspoon cayenne pepper
2 teaspoons mustard powder
1 teaspoon ground turmeric
6 tablespoons sunflower oil
450 g/1 lb sweet potato, cubed
450 g/1 lb peeled and cubed pumpkin or squash

4 tablespoons dark rum
250 ml/9 fl oz stock
2 large plantains, peeled and sliced into rounds about 1 cm/½ inch thick
400 ml/14 fl oz coconut milk
salt and pepper
juice of 1 lime
chopped oregano leaves, to garnish
mango slices, to serve
chives, snipped into longish pieces, to garnish

SERVES 4–6

In a food processor, blend the onions, garlic and ginger to a paste. Using a spice grinder or mortar and pestle, grind the coriander seeds, cloves and cinnamon. Add the cayenne, mustard powder and turmeric.

Heat 4 tablespoons of the oil in a saucepan, add the onion paste and fry for 2 minutes. Add the sweet potato and pumpkin or squash, and fry until they start to soften. Now add the spices and stir. Add the rum, followed by the stock. Cover and bring to the boil. Simmer with the lid on until the vegetables are soft. Add a little water, as necessary.

Meanwhile, fry the plantain in the remaining oil, until brown and crunchy. Add the plantain to the saucepan with the coconut milk, and simmer gently for 5 minutes. Finally add salt to taste and the lime juice.

Serve garnished with chopped oregano leaves, accompanied by the slices of fresh mango sprinkled with chives and some rice.

MEXICO

The Mexican state of Oaxaca is a land of rugged mountains, ancient Zapotec and Mixtec ruins, Indian markets and winding valleys around the preserved colonial gem of Cortes' southern capital of Oaxaca city. At the same time, as one of Mexico's west-coast states, it offers in places such as Puerto Escondido a very modern culture that owes little to its Aztec or its Spanish past.

The city of Oaxaca is centred on the *zocalo* (square), a leafy oasis of shade surrounded by cafés under stone arcades. At night each café has its own band of musicians to serenade customers, and street vendors offer bright plastic toys, giant balloons, multicoloured jellies, and armloads of hand-knitted shawls. Every day at dawn and dusk, café society on the *zocalo* is silenced by a flamboyant display of nationalism as a troop of highly polished soldiers attends with great seriousness to the hoisting or lowering of the Mexican flag.

Beyond the *zocalo*, Oaxaca still retains much of its historic Andalusian charm. There are some fine sixteenth-century churches, most impressive of which is Santo Domingo, with its lavish gold-leaf interior where a mass or even a wedding will carry on oblivious to the gaze of visitors. The town is dotted with colonial haciendas constructed around tranquil courtyards; some of these have been converted into hotels and guest-houses, and we stayed in a charming example for several days.

Oaxaca's cuisine is part of the town's image and features heavily in its restaurants. Oaxaqueño, a stringy, mozzarella-style cheese, and mole, a rich, spicy chocolate and herb sauce, are both common. Slightly less so are *chapulines*, fried grasshoppers, which, even when cooked with onion and garlic and served with fresh lime, looked like an acquired taste. Most of the ingredients, including piles of grasshoppers and blocks of raw chocolate, are on display in the Mercado de Abastos. In typical Mexican style, the market is a colourful labyrinth of stalls and shops, full of treats (and occasional horrors) for the eyes, nose and stomach.

To the east of Oaxaca we visited several ruins of Zapotec settlements, at Mitla enjoying a rare opportunity to see reasonably intact examples of original stone mosaic-work in geometric designs representing the elements — designs that are now used by weavers and potters. For all its subtle attractions, however, Mitla has none of the dramatic grandeur of its historic predecessor Monte Albán. The ruins of this ancient city are majestically located just west of Oaxaca and 400 metres (1,320 ft) above it. Monte Albán at its peak, around 2,000 years ago, was home to 25,000 Zapotec inhabitants.

Blocks of chocolate for making mole on sale in the market in Oaxaca

The most visible legacy of the settlement's architectural triumph is the flattened mountain-top on which the ruins stand. The mountain was levelled by hand to make a vast, paved plateau. Around the edge temples, tombs, palaces, platforms and pyramids were constructed, and enough of them remain to make Monte Albán one of Mexico's finest relics of pre-Hispanic civilization.

From Oaxaca we took an eight-seater plane back over the Sierra Madre to the coast to indulge in the relaxed pleasures of Puerto Escondido. The size and power of the waves along Zicatela beach make a compelling spectacle, and attract surfers from all over the Americas. Surfing culture is also entertaining to observe. Surfing is a mainly male sport on Zicatela, and there is much strutting and posing to watch, as well as some extraordinary acrobatics and daring. The atmosphere is easy-going and international. Puerto Escondido has none of the modern high-rise hotels found along the coast in Huatulco, nor is it as remote and laid-back as the sleepy fishing village and one-time hippy hideaway of Puerto Angel half-way between the two. Puerto Angel offers the ultimate wind-down after all the activity and urban formality of Oaxaca, and a chance to experience the Mexican *mañana* mood to the full.

GUACAMOLE

SMOOTH GUACAMOLE

SERVES 4–6

> 4 large ripe avocados (preferably Hass)
>
> 1 jalapeño chilli, roughly chopped
>
> small handful of coriander leaves, chopped, plus more for garnish
>
> juice of 1 lime
>
> salt
>
> tortilla chips, to serve

Halve the avocados and stone them. Scoop out the flesh and put it into a food processor. Add all the remaining ingredients and blend until smooth.

Serve garnished with chopped coriander leaves, accompanied by tortilla chips.

CHOPPED GUACAMOLE

SERVES 4–6

> 3 large ripe avocados (preferably Hass)
>
> 2 medium tomatoes, finely diced
>
> 1 small red onion, finely chopped
>
> juice of 1 lime
>
> salt
>
> chopped coriander leaves, for garnish
>
> tortilla chips, to serve

Peel and stone the avocados. Chop the flesh, place in a bowl and mush slightly with a fork. Now add all the remaining ingredients and mix well.

Serve garnished with chopped coriander leaves, accompanied by tortilla chips.

There are many different versions of guacamole, a delicious avocado salsa. It can be served smooth or with chopped avocado, so we've given you both options. You can serve it either as an appetizer or as an accompaniment.

Chopped Guacamole

This truly original dish combines chocolate and spices to make a rich, dark, savoury sauce. We were taught this recipe by a woman from Oaxaca market. She cooked everything on open fires in her courtyard, which her husband and sons also used as a mechanic's workshop. From tins and jars on shelves above dismantled engines and buckets of sump oil she produced the dried ingredients, which she blended with the chocolate and other items to create the mole. We thanked her so enthusiastically for her trouble that she invited us to join her and the grinning mechanics for lunch. As our cookery lesson had been conducted next to an evil-smelling pot containing a boiling pig's head we politely declined.

OAXACAN MOLE

It is best to use a chocolate with a high cocoa content.

SERVES 4–6

500 g/1 lb 2 oz sweet potatoes, cut into 2.5 cm/1 inch cubes

2 sweetcorn cobs, cut into 2.5 cm/1 inch rounds

salt

4 tablespoons sunflower oil

2 plantains, peeled and cut into 1 cm/½ inch rounds

1 red and 1 yellow pepper, deseeded and cut into 2.5 cm/1 inch squares

125 g/4 oz green beans

For the mole sauce

30 g/1 oz roasted shelled peanuts

30 g/1 oz sesame seeds

30 g/1 oz pumpkin seeds

5 cm/2 inch piece of cinnamon stick

60 g/2 oz ground almonds

1 level teaspoon ground allspice

½ teaspoon ground cloves

1 teaspoon dried thyme

1 level tablespoon dried oregano

1 onion, roughly chopped

3 garlic cloves

2 jalapeño chillies

60 g/2 oz raisins

1 medium banana, peeled and roughly chopped

3 tablespoons sunflower oil

300 ml/½ pint stock

125 g/4 oz plain chocolate

First make the mole sauce: grind the peanuts, sesame seeds, pumpkin seeds and cinnamon in a food processor. Add the ground almonds, allspice, cloves, thyme and oregano, onion, garlic, chillies, raisins and banana. Blend to a thick paste.

Heat the sunflower oil in a large pan and, when hot, add the paste and fry for 2 minutes, stirring constantly. Slowly add the stock, stirring well.

Break up the chocolate and add to the sauce. Stir well until the chocolate has melted. Simmer gently for 10 minutes. The sauce will be quite thick.

Now prepare the vegetables: parboil the sweet potato and sweetcorn in boiling salted water for about 1–2 minutes. Drain well.

Heat the sunflower oil in a pan. When it is hot, add the plantains and fry until they start to brown. Add the sweet potato, sweetcorn and peppers, and fry until they all start to brown.

Stir the fried vegetables into the mole sauce, then add the green beans and 200 ml/7 fl oz water. Simmer gently for 10 minutes. Season with salt to taste.

REFRIED BEANS

When cooking pulses it is important not to add salt until the end as salt stops the pulses from softening properly.

SERVES 4–6

425 g/15 oz pinto beans, soaked in
    water overnight
1 level tablespoon cumin seeds
1 level tablespoon coriander seeds

4 tablespoons sunflower oil
1 large onion, finely chopped
salt

Drain and rinse the beans. Place in a large saucepan with enough fresh water to cover. Bring to the boil. A foam will rise to the surface of the pan – simply scoop off and discard. Cover the pan and simmer until beans are nice and soft.

Meanwhile, dry-roast the cumin and coriander seeds in a hot frying pan for 1 minute, stirring constantly. Grind in a grinder or using a pestle and mortar. Set aside.

Heat the sunflower oil in a frying pan and, when hot, fry the onion gently until soft (but not brown or it becomes bitter). Add the ground spices and fry with the onion for 1 minute, stirring constantly.

Add the onion mixture to the pan of soft pinto beans. Remove from the heat and mash with a potato masher until the beans are broken down and viscous. If necessary, add more water to get a thick porridge-like consistency. Finally add salt to taste.

Beans are the staple of most Mexican meals. Refried beans are the most common and can be served with almost anything – the options are endless. They can be made with various beans, but pinto or black beans are the most common. We prefer to use pinto beans. In the café we serve refried beans in a flour tortilla and as part of a mixed Mexican plate.

Above left **A colourful Oaxacan street**
Above **Hats for sale in the town of Mérida**

REFRIED BEANS WITH FLOUR TORTILLA

SERVES 1

1 serving of Refried Beans
1 soft flour tortilla
handful of grated mature Cheddar
    cheese
blob of sour cream

For the mixed salad
finely shredded lettuce

grated carrot
finely shredded red cabbage
finely shredded white cabbage
coriander leaves, chopped, to garnish

For the salad dressing
lime juice
olive oil

Reheat the refried beans. Combine all the salad ingredients and dress with the lime juice and olive oil. Sprinkle with the coriander.

Toast the soft flour tortilla on a hot griddle or in a hot dry frying pan until it starts to puff up. Turn and cover with grated cheese. When the cheese starts to melt, transfer to a plate dressed with the salad. Spoon the beans on the tortilla and fold it in half. Place a blob of sour cream on top and serve immediately.

MEXICAN PLATE WITH REFRIED BEANS

SERVES 1

mixed salad as above
Fresh Tomato Salsa (page 176) or
    Salsa Ranchera (page 175)
Smooth Guacamole (page 168)
blob of sour cream

1 serving of Refried Beans
handful of grated mature Cheddar
    cheese
coriander leaves, chopped, to garnish
tortilla chips, to serve

Arrange the salad over half of each plate and top it with servings of salsa, guacamole and sour cream. Cover the remaining side of the plate with refried beans and top these with grated Cheddar cheese.

Garnish with chopped coriander leaves and place lots of tortilla chips around the edge of the plate. Serve immediately.

CHAYOTE IN A CINNAMON-SPICED TOMATO SAUCE

The chayote or chow chow, a vegetable enjoyed right across Mexico, is now available in many supermarkets and specialist shops. Resembling a large green pear, it is similar to the marrow in texture. The seed in the middle is considered a delicacy so, when chopping the chayote, use it all. If you cannot find chayote, use marrow instead. When chayote is in season, we like to serve this dish garnished with courgette flowers lightly fried in butter together with mashed sweet potato to soak up the sauce.

SERVES 4–6

3 chayote, peeled with a potato peeler and chopped into cubes, or 675 g / 1½ lb peeled and cubed marrow

5 baby courgettes, halved lengthwise

salt and pepper

For the tomato sauce

4 tablespoons olive oil

1 large onion, diced

3 garlic cloves, crushed

1 teaspoon ground cinnamon

¼ teaspoon ground cloves

1 tablespoon tomato purée

450 g / 1 lb tomatoes, finely diced

handful of raisins

large handful of coriander leaves, chopped

2 jalapeño chillies, chopped

For the garnish (optional)

12 courgette flowers

butter, for frying

First make the tomato sauce: heat the olive oil in a saucepan and, when hot, fry the onion and garlic gently until soft. Stir the cinnamon and cloves into the onions, then add the tomato purée, diced tomatoes, raisins, chopped coriander and chillies, together with a little water to loosen the sauce. Simmer for 10 minutes.

Now prepare the vegetables: parboil the chayote or marrow and the courgettes in salted water until they start to soften. Drain and stir them into the sauce. Simmer gently for 15 minutes. Add salt and pepper to taste.

If courgette flowers are in season, gently fry them in butter until they start to brown. Season to taste.

Serve the dish garnished with the courgette flowers, if you have them, and accompanied by sweet potato mashed with olive oil and chopped fresh thyme.

On Saturdays the streets and alleyways around the *mercado* in Oaxaca fill with Zapotec Indians from the surrounding countryside selling their produce from the pavement. As well as everyday goods, there are numerous Indian crafts on sale, including hundreds of blankets and rugs woven with traditional geometric patterns and coloured with dyes such as cochineal and indigo.

Best of all, there's plenty of street food freshly prepared between the stalls to feed hungry shoppers. As well as lots of warm Oaxaqueño tortillas with various salsas, we ate a very good dish made with chayote, or chow chow, in a tomato, clove and cinnamon sauce spiced with jalapeños and garlic.

When you order your food in Mexico you will generally be asked if you would like red or green salsa. These are cooked salsas and are used to sauce your food. Take as little or as much as you like, but no meal is complete without one.

Our favourite is the red salsa known as salsa ranchera. A green version can be made by replacing tomatoes with tomatillos, which look like green tomatoes and are occasionally available in good supermarkets or specialist shops. Salsa ranchera is also an ingredient in a favourite recipe of ours, Huevos Rancheros.

SALSA RANCHERA

SERVES 4–6

1–2 tablespoons sunflower oil
1 red onion, finely chopped
1 garlic clove, crushed
1–2 jalapeño chillies, finely chopped

handful of fresh coriander, chopped
6 medium tomatoes, finely diced
salt

Heat the oil in a small pan and, when hot, fry onion and garlic until starting to soften. Stir in the chillies and coriander and cook for a further few seconds. Now add the chopped tomatoes and gently simmer until all the ingredients are soft and well cooked down. Season to taste with salt.

This salsa can be stored in the fridge for up to 2 weeks.

HUEVOS RANCHEROS

Basically fried eggs served on a flour tortilla and covered in spicy ranchera sauce, this makes not only a delicious breakfast dish but also a wonderful lunch.

SERVES 1

1–2 soft flour tortillas
1–2 eggs
1 tablespoon olive oil
Salsa Ranchera, as much or as little as you like, but enough to cover the egg

handful of grated mature hard cheese, such as Cheddar
coriander leaves, chopped, to garnish

On a hot griddle or in a hot dry frying pan, cook the soft flour tortillas until they start to puff up. Flip them over and toast the other side.

Meanwhile, fry the eggs in the oil, keeping the yolk soft. Heat the ranchera sauce.

Now assemble the dish. Place a fried egg on top of each toasted tortilla and cover with the ranchera sauce. Sprinkle with the grated cheese and chopped coriander leaves. Serve immediately.

FRESH TOMATO SALSA

This fresh tomato salsa is often eaten with tortilla chips as an appetizer. It is also good served with refried beans.

SERVES 4–6

1 small red onion, roughly chopped.
1–2 jalapeño chillies
large handful of coriander, chopped,
    plus more to garnish
5 medium ripe tomatoes, roughly
    chopped

juice of 2 limes
salt
tortilla chips, to serve

Blend the onion, chillies and coriander in a food processor until finely chopped (you can do this by hand if you prefer). Now add the tomatoes, lime juice and salt to taste, then briefly blend again until the tomato is finely chopped and blended with all ingredients – but not turned to tomato juice.

Serve garnished with more chopped coriander leaves and accompanied by tortilla chips, or as an accompaniment to any meal.

FRESH TOMATO AND RADISH SALSA

This is a chunkier salsa, which again may be served with tortilla chips or to accompany any meal.

SERVES 4–6

4 medium tomatoes, finely diced
1 small red onion, finely diced
1 bunch of radishes, sliced
small handful of coriander leaves,
    chopped

juice of 1 lime
salt
1 small green chilli, finely chopped

Mix all the ingredients with salt to taste.

As well as the cooked salsas served as condiments, there are various fresh salsas made with raw ingredients, which may be served as an appetizer or as an accompaniment to the main dish.

Fresh Tomato and
Radish Salsa

Surfers in the sunset at
Puerto Escondido

FRESH FRUIT SALSA

*In Oaxaca city, market stalls are piled high with the most beautiful fruits – papaya,
watermelon and cantaloupe melon are but a few – and these are often used to make a
spicy salsa.*

SERVES 4–6

60 g/2 oz pumpkin seeds	juice of 2 limes
450 g/1 lb papaya, watermelon,	handful of coriander leaves
galia melon or cantaloupe melon,	1 jalapeño chilli, finely chopped
or a mix of all four, peeled,	salt
deseeded and cut into small cubes	

Toast the pumpkin seeds in a hot dry frying pan until they become golden,
stirring constantly. Set aside to cool.

    Mix your choice of fruit with the lime juice, coriander and chilli. Season
with salt to taste and cover with the toasted pumpkin seeds.

In Puerto Escondido New Age Californian culture blends with local Oaxacan youth culture on the surf beaches and in their cafés. This blend has crept into the food. The beach cafés open at dawn to serve surfers as much with muesli, fresh fruit and yoghurt as with huevos rancheros. By midday the choice expands to all manner of vegetarian, fish and meat dishes. Many cafés serve Indonesian tempeh. The recipe given here combines tempeh with colourful peppers, olives and that Mexican staple, pinto beans.

MEXICAN WEST COAST PEPPERS

SERVES 4–6

5 tablespoons olive oil
300 g / 10 oz tempeh, cut into 1 cm / ½ inch cubes
2 red onions, thinly sliced
4 garlic cloves, sliced
2 red chillies, chopped
2 tablespoons coriander seeds, crushed

2 red peppers, 2 yellow peppers and 1 green pepper, deseeded and sliced
350 g / 12 oz cooked pinto beans
24 black olives, stoned and halved
soy sauce
large handful of coriander leaves, chopped

Heat half the oil in a large pan and, when hot, fry the tempeh until brown. Remove from pan and set aside.

Add the remaining oil to the pan and, when hot, fry the onion until it starts to soften. Add the garlic, chilli and crushed coriander seeds. Fry for a couple of minutes.

Add the peppers and fry, stirring regularly, until they start to soften. Add the pinto beans and olives. When the beans are heated through, return the tempeh to the pan and stir well.

Add soy sauce to taste and the chopped coriander. Serve immediately with Fresh Fruit Salsa (page 178) and rice.

CUBA

There was only one flight a week between London and Havana in the winter of 1994, and that was on a rather old and ill-equipped Russian aeroplane operated by Cubana out of Stansted Airport. The lack of in-flight entertainment was partly compensated for by the freely available Havana Club rum. The biggest shock was a stopover in the frozen north of Canada, where we had to endure sub-zero temperatures as we walked to and from the terminal building dressed for the Caribbean in T-shirts and sandals.

It can be uncomfortable arriving in a strange city at night with no accommodation booked. But, far from being besieged by taxi-drivers competing to whisk us into the unknown for a huge fare, we found the Havana Airport taxi-men playing guitars under a tree in the tropical evening. After a sedate drive down almost empty roads at a fixed fare to the heart of Old Havana, we found a fine room in a hotel rich, like Havana itself, in faded splendour. The elegant Spanish colonial architecture, the brightly coloured 1950s American cars, the post-revolutionary street art, the subtle pastels of the back alleys, and the friendly Cuban people — all made photography a pleasure. Eating was another matter. Seduced into restaurants by stunning interiors and smiling staff, we inevitably found nothing to back up the optimistic words on the menus, while the big hotels seemed content to serve dishes reminiscent of boarding-school meals of the 1960s. We were beginning to despair when rescue came from what seemed a most unlikely source.

At first we had been rather intimidated by the gangs of young men hustling to sell dodgy merchandise in the shadows. But after a couple of days we discovered that they were much less threatening than they appeared, and in fact quite friendly and keen to chat in English. Having turned down their suggestions of various substances to smoke, sniff or sip we found there was something else on offer. A boy who introduced himself as José was our guide to this elusive pleasure. Reluctant at first to follow him down the quiet, narrow streets into the midst of Old Havana's decay, we nonetheless stayed close behind him, drawn by his promise of tasty, home-cooked Cuban dishes for a few dollars.

José introduced us to Rosa, his aunt. Rosa was an old hand at saving foreigners from Havana's dearth of nutritious satisfaction. With her passion for traditional Cuban cooking, she provided some of our most pleasant and enduring memories of Cuba. After her delicious meals we would spend the warm Havana nights sipping Mojito rum cocktails in one of the foodless bars or cafés, followed by live Afro-Cuban dance music at an open-air club, against a background of Atlantic waves crashing on the shore.

One of the many big
old American cars to
be seen on the streets
of Havana

CUBAN GREEN RICE

<small>SERVES 4–6</small>

3 tablespoons olive oil
1 large onion, finely chopped
1 green pepper, deseeded and finely
    chopped
large handful of fresh parsley,
    chopped

large handful of fresh coriander
    leaves, chopped
500 g/1 lb 2 oz rice, rinsed
about 700 ml/1¼ pints stock
salt and pepper

Heat the oil in the saucepan in which you are going to cook the rice. When hot, fry the onion and pepper until they start to soften.

Stir in the chopped parsley and coriander. Add the drained rice and stir to coat all the grains in oil. Add just enough stock to cover the rice and bring to the boil, then reduce the heat and cook with the lid on until all the moisture is absorbed. Adjust the seasoning if necessary.

A pot in a Havana
street forms a casual
still-life.

HAVANA BEANS

Serves 4–6

325 g/11 oz black beans, soaked
    overnight in cold water

6 tablespoons olive oil

2 large red onions, thinly sliced

6 garlic cloves, crushed

2 red peppers, deseeded and thinly
    sliced

2 yellow peppers, deseeded and
    thinly sliced

450 g/1 lb white cabbage, finely
    shredded

large handful of coriander stalks,
    chopped, and a large handful of
    chopped coriander leaves

large handful of chopped oregano
    leaves, plus more to garnish

Tabasco sauce

5 tablespoons red wine

salt and pepper

For the garnish

slices of plum tomato

chopped fresh oregano

olive oil

Drain the soaked black beans, add enough fresh water to cover generously, bring
to the boil and simmer until soft. Drain the beans, retaining the cooking liquor.

Meanwhile, heat 4 tablespoons of the olive oil in a large pan and, when hot,
fry the red onions and garlic. When they start to soften, add the red and yellow
peppers, followed shortly thereafter by the cabbage. Fry, stirring constantly,
until the vegetables are nice and soft, and caramelized.

Add the coriander stalks, oregano and Tabasco to taste – it should be quite
spicy! Stir well and add the wine. When the wine has reduced by about half, add
the cooked beans and the remaining olive oil, followed by enough of the
reserved bean cooking liquor to make a sauce. Simmer for 5 minutes.

Finally add salt and pepper to taste and the chopped coriander leaves. Stir
until well incorporated.

Serve immediately, garnished with chopped oregano leaves, and
accompanied by Cuban Green Rice (page 181) and plump plum tomato slices
drizzled with olive oil.

CHOCOLATE CAKE

In nearly all the countries we have travelled in, the most common dessert is fresh fruit. However, in the café we serve a French chocolate cake, which is probably our most requested recipe. Up to now we have always tried to keep it a secret, but this book would not be complete without it.

SERVES 8–10

225 g/8 oz unsalted butter, plus more for the cake pan

200 g/7 oz plain chocolate, broken into pieces

6 large eggs, separated

200 g/7 oz caster sugar

icing sugar, for dusting

crème fraîche, to serve

strawberries, to serve

Preheat the oven to 190°/375°F/gas 5 and grease a 23 cm/9 inch loose-bottomed cake tin well with butter (the cake mixture can be runny, so it is best to use the type of pan that is tightly secured by a clip).

In a small saucepan set over a larger pan of simmering water, melt the chocolate and the butter. Mix together well and set aside to cool.

Meanwhile, using a whisk – preferably in a food mixer – beat the egg whites until really stiff. While still whisking, slowly add the caster sugar followed by the egg yolks. The result should be a creamy mixture.

Using a metal spoon, quickly combine the chocolate butter sauce with this cake mixture. Pour and spoon into the prepared cake tin.

Bake for approximately 55 minutes. The cake will puff up in the oven but will sink back down again when removed from the heat, to give it its characteristic appearance.

Dust with lots of icing sugar and serve with crème fraîche and strawberries.

Chocolate Cake

GLOSSARY OF INGREDIENTS

amchoor Made from ground dried unripe mango, this powder gives food a sweet sourness. It is available from Indian stores.

asafoetida See *hing*.

bindi See *okra*.

black bean paste A paste of puréed, salted and fermented soya beans, available from good supermarkets or Chinese stores. Alternatively you can buy the black beans whole, rinse them and purée them with some water.

'Buddhist meat' A delicious meat substitute made from marinated wheat gluten, this is available from health-food stores under the name of seitan.

bulghur (bulgar) wheat Cracked kernels of wheat, available in fine or medium coarseness (we prefer fine). It can be bought from good supermarkets or health-food stores.

cardamom Aromatic pods containing either green or black seeds. Remove the seeds from the pod for maximum flavour; alternatively it is possible to buy the seeds or ground seeds only.

cassava A Brazilian root vegetable similar to a large sweet potato but with a darker skin. Its flesh is hard and white, but becomes glutinous when cooked.

coconut milk Available canned, powdered or creamed. We like the canned form best. It is thicker than the powdered version and less likely to separate on being cooked. If you do use the powder, always mix it to a consistency thicker than that suggested on the packet. The creamed coconut, sold in blocks, tends to be rather oily.

creamed tomatoes A preparation of smooth, thick, sieved tomatoes, available from good supermarkets, delicatessens and health-food stores.

curry leaves Highly aromatic leaves much used in Indian cooking. Shaped like small bay leaves, they are much better fresh than dried, and fresh leaves can be bought from Indian stores. Dried are available from supermarket spice counters. Curry leaves can be frozen.

daikon See *mooli*.

galangal This root, a member of the ginger family, is available fresh or dried from Thai, Chinese or Malaysian stores. If necessary, root ginger makes a good substitute.

ghee Well-clarified butter, used in Indian cooking and available from Indian stores or good supermarkets. It is possible to buy a dairy-free version.

gram flour Made from ground chickpeas, this flour is available from good supermarkets or Indian stores.

hing Also known as asafoetida, this pungent resin flavouring, ground into a yellow powder, is available from Indian stores.

hoisin sauce A dark-brown, sweet, smooth Chinese bean sauce, available from good supermarkets or Chinese stores.

jaggery Lump brown sugar from a type of palm tree, jaggery is sold in blocks in Indian stores or the ethnic sections of good supermarkets.

jalapeño chillies The most commonly used chillies in Mexico, these are available fresh, dried or canned in brine, from good super-markets or specialist shops. Jalapeño chillies are large and quite hot; if using regular chillies double the quantity.

lemon grass These hard, thick, pale-green stalks are much used in Southeast Asian cooking. Their distinctive lemon flavour is best brought out by bruising the stalks with a rolling pin before adding them to the pot. It is possible to buy lemon grass fresh, freeze-dried whole, or dried and sliced or dried and ground. If you use dried, 2 tablespoons is equivalent to 1 stalk; but try to use fresh when possible. Lemon grass stalks can be frozen, so stock up your freezer whenever you can. They are available from good supermarkets and Chinese, Thai or Malaysian stores.

lime leaves The leaves of the kaffir lime tree, widely used in Southeast Asian cooking. They are available from Thai, Chinese or Malaysian stores.

mooli A large white radish with a mild flavour, available from good supermarkets and Chinese or Thai stores. Also known as daikon.

mung dal Split mung beans, available from Indian stores.

okra Finger-length, green, pod-like vegetables, also known as bindi, and available from good supermarkets and Indian, Chinese or Thai stores.

paneer An Indian fresh cheese, white in colour and available in blocks from good supermarkets or Indian stores. Quite bland on its own, paneer is tasty when cooked in sauces.

pinto beans These medium-sized dried beans flecked with brown and pink are available from health-food stores or good supermarkets.

plantain This tropical fruit looks like a large thick-skinned green banana and it is related to the banana, although it is quite different in flavour and texture.

rosewater Water flavoured with roses is available from Middle Eastern stores, delicatessens or good supermarkets.

seitan See 'Buddhist meat'.

tahini (tahina) A thick paste made from ground hulled sesame seeds, and available from health-food stores, good supermarkets, delicatessens or Middle Eastern stores

tamarind These brown pods used as a sour flavouring can be bought dried or as a ready-made purée or concentrate. We prefer tamarind purée, which is available from good supermarkets, Indian stores or health-food shops. Tamarind concentrate is indeed much more concentrated and half the quantity stated in the recipe is usually sufficient. If you can only get the dried pods, soak them in boiling water for 1 hour, or gently simmer them in water until soft, then pass through a sieve to collect the tamarind water and pulp. Use both, discarding the pods and the pips.

tempeh A nutty-flavoured brown block made from soya beans, available from health-food or Indonesian stores.

tofu Made from set soya beancurd, tofu is available in many forms, including soft, hard, deep-fried, marinated and smoked. We like to use deep-fried tofu as it has more flavour and needs little cooking.

tortillas, flour Soft Mexican pancakes, tortillas are at the centre of most Mexican meals. They are available from good supermarkets, delicatessens or health-food stores.

INDEX

ACKNOWLEDGMENTS

Many people have helped to make this book happen, whether by creating opportunities, offering hospitality, giving recipes or sharing adventures. We especially wish to thank Nigel de Winser, Joana Scadden, Cecilia Weston-Baker, John Grain, Kirsty Seymour-Ure, Donna and Simon Leibowitz, Christine Dunk, Sally Cracknell, Vicky Mitchell, Satish Jacob and family, Vijayendra Singh and family, Kishori and Kalpa Shah, John and Richard Hunt, Robert Spensly, Daniel Tucker, Sophie Chamier and Giles Caldicott.

Map of the world copyright © AND Cartographic Publishers Ltd.

Commissioning Editor
Jo Christian

Managing Art Editor
Jo Grey

Text Editor
Kirsty Seymour-Ure

Art Editor
John Grain

Recipe Editor
Lewis Esson

Food Styling
Nicola Fowler

Editorial Assistance
Tom Armstrong and
Tom Windross

Production
Hazel Kirkman

Picture Editor
Anne Fraser

Indexer
Roger Owen

Art Director
Caroline Hillier

Editorial Director
Kate Cave

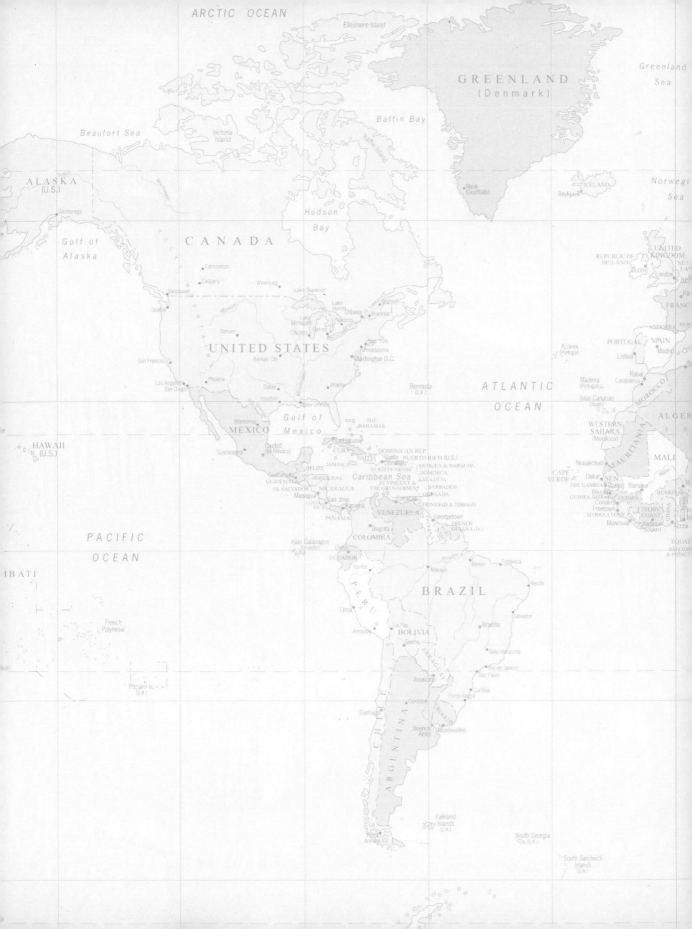